THE QUICK START BEGINNER'S GUIDE TO THE BIBLE

J. STEPHEN LANG

HARVEST HOUSE PUBLISHERS

EUGENE, OREGON

ΜΒ

Unless otherwise indicated, all Scripture quotations are taken from the HOLY BIBLE, NEW INTER-
NATIONAL VERSION ®. NIV ®. Copyright © 1973, 1978, 1984 by the International Bible Society.
Used by permission of Zondervan. All rights reserved.

Verses marked KJV are taken from the King James Version of the Bible.

Verses marked GNT (TEV) are taken from the Good News Translation—Second Edition © 1992 by
American Bible Society. Used by permission.

Published in association with the literary agency of Mark Sweeney & Associates, 28540 Altessa Way,
Suite 201, Bonita Springs, FL 34135

Cover by Terry Dugan Design, Minneapolis, Minnesota

Cover photo © Jill Fromer / iStockphoto

THE QUICK-START BEGINNER'S GUIDE TO THE BIBLE
Copyright © 2007 by J. Stephen Lang
Published by Harvest House Publishers
Eugene, Oregon 97402

Library of Congress Cataloging-in-Publication Data
   Lang, J. Stephen.
   The quick-start beginner's guide to the Bible / J. Stephen Lang
      p. cm.
   ISBN-13: 978-0-7369-1938-8 (pbk.)
   ISBN-10: 0-7369-1938-4
   1. Bible—Introductions I. Title.
   BS475.3.L36 2007
   220.6'1—dc22

                                                        2006031308

CONTENTS

MAKING THE
BIBLE
USER-FRIENDLY

Here in the twenty-first century, can an ancient book be user-friendly? Can the life of King David, who lived around 1000 B.C., be accessible, or interesting, or relevant to contemporary individuals?

Granted, the Bible isn't as accessible as the Internet or MTV. It isn't supposed to be. It's the Word of God to human beings, not a multi-image promo for throwaway pop culture. The Bible is serious. It's concerned with morality, with ethics, with values. It's concerned with where we came from, how we should live, what our destiny is beyond this present life. In other words, it answers the basic human questions about the meaning of life.

But it *is* accessible. And it is interesting. If sex and violence help sell books and videos, then the Bible should sell well, for sex and violence are there. (Mark Twain snickered at libraries that banned his books but kept the Bible on their shelves.) The Bible presents the human tale, warts and all—and adds the divine element, making the picture complete. It's even more interesting than pop culture because it has everything the secular world has, *plus* a loving, forgiving, saving God. The Almighty God is, according to the Bible, approachable—friendly, if you will.

User-friendly means that an average, normal human being can approach without feeling threatened. Bible handbooks flood the market—and many seem to assume that the reader already knows the Bible fairly well and enjoys reading it. The book you are now holding assumes no such thing. It assumes you are at least *interested* in the Bible—maybe slightly familiar with it, but maybe puzzled, curious, perhaps even hostile. It doesn't assume you know the order of the Bible's books, its main characters, its key teachings, its history, or its place in everyday life. It does assume that knowledge of these things is important—as important as knowing how to drive a car, program a video recorder, operate a microwave oven, fill out a tax return, or shop for nutritious food. In fact, this book assumes that knowing the Bible is *more* important than all these things. Yet it does not assume you must be a scholar or a college grad to know the Bible.

This book is written for several types of people:

- The new Christian who wants to become familiar with the Book of books, which is the foundation of Christian belief and living. The new believer can profit from studying this handbook alone, but I encourage group study when possible. Church and home classes or groups should find this book eminently user-friendly.

- The person who wants to get "reacquainted"—that is, the person who realizes he has neglected the Bible for too long and would like to become more familiar with it. Surveys consistently show that longtime churchgoers are often ignorant of basic Bible teachings. I hope this book will help to remedy that problem.

- The Christian who is familiar with the Bible but would like a refresher course, a kind of review of Bible 101, if you will. Pastors and professors often fall into this category.

- The non-Christian who is curious—curious as a seeker after truth, or maybe as one who opposes Christianity but wonders if the failings of Christianity are traceable to the Bible itself. For the seeker, I hope this book leads to further inquiry and commitment. For the hostile person, I hope at least to clarify. Certainly I include nothing here that should make a non-Christian *less* respectful of the Bible and Christianity.

Several years ago I published *The Complete Book of Bible Trivia.* It has sold extremely well, which made me realize that a lot of people are interested in the "tidbits" of the Bible, its many interesting snippets of events, people, and places. Having looked at the Bible as *trivia,* I now move on to *significa*—the Bible as something that is, or can be, very significant in human life. My trivia book answered the question, Can the Bible entertain me? The book you are now holding answers the question, The Bible—what's in it for me?

1

Beyond the Words:

WHAT IS THE BIBLE ALL ABOUT?

Bibles are sold by the millions every year across the globe. Are they being read? Some are, some aren't. If the sales figures meant anything, we would be a very Bible-literate people. But that isn't so.

It *was* so—in the past, anyway. If you read the history of the United States and England, you can't help but notice that great leaders of the past often quoted and referred to the Bible. Even when their actions were morally questionable, they were at least familiar with what the Bible taught. It was a part of education, just like learning the mythology of Greece and Rome, but more important than mythology because most people believed the Bible was *true*. Even people who questioned the miraculous elements in the Bible—Thomas Jefferson was one, for example—still believed that its moral and ethical teachings applied to human life. They believed that God in some way produced the Bible. Thus it wasn't just a book, such as a novel by Charles Dickens or a long poem such as *The Odyssey*. It had its origin in God wanting to reveal his will to the human race. People often claimed that they had "heard" God speaking to them individually. The general belief about the Bible was that it was God speaking to everyone who could read it or hear it being read aloud.

The word *Bible* simply means "the book." One modern version was even marketed as *The Book,* which is accurate. But the Bible doesn't have one author in the same way most books have one author. It was written over a span of hundreds of years by many different people. Each author had—as all authors do—an individual way of expressing himself in words. No two books of the Bible are exactly alike, even the ones by the same author.

What Are These "Books"?

Before we look deeper into the Bible, let's consider some terminology. Pastors and teachers talk about a particular "book" of the Bible. Meaning what? Each section of the Bible—there are 66 in all—is called a book, even though none of them is big enough to fill an entire book by itself. Thus we talk about the book of Psalms and the book of Jeremiah and the book of Acts. Most of these books fill up many pages (the longest one is the book of Psalms), but some are smaller (the book of Obadiah barely fills a page). So a book doesn't mean "something between two covers," but "a component part." Each book is divided into chapters and verses (more about these divisions later), and most of the books are attributed to a single author. The book of Acts, for example, is supposed to have been written by Luke (who also wrote the Gospel of Luke), and the book of Revelation was written by John. Some books have several authors. Psalms, for example, was written by King David and some others. Proverbs was written by King Solomon, Agur, Lemuel, and possibly others.

In some cases a particular book may have been edited. The book of Deuteronomy in the Old Testament is supposed to have been written by Moses, but at its end it tells about Moses' death, so we have to assume that someone else edited the book and added the material about Moses' death at the end.

As mentioned earlier, *Bible* simply means "the book." For people who accept it as divine, it is *the* Book, the most important book of all.

What Are the Books Named For?

The 66 books of the Bible are named a variety of ways. In the New Testament, the four Gospels—the stories of Jesus—are named for their different authors (Matthew, Mark, Luke, John). So are the Old Testament prophetic books, such as Isaiah, Ezekiel, and Amos. And so are some parts of the New Testament (the epistles, or letters, of Peter, James, and John). Some books are named for their main character, who may or may not be the author. Some examples are Joshua, Ruth, Esther, Job, and Ezra.

The book of Acts is named for its content (it tells of the acts, or deeds, of the early Christians). So are the books of Revelation (it is a "revealing" of the future) and Exodus (it concerns the exodus, or exit, of the people of Israel from Egypt). Some books are named for their intended audience. This is true of most of the epistles or letters in the New Testament, which are addressed to, for example, the Romans, the Colossians, the Ephesians, and to individuals such as Timothy and Titus.

Some books seem to be named wrongly. For example, Numbers (the fourth book of the Old Testament) tells about a census, but this is only a tiny part of the book. And some names—Leviticus, Deuteronomy, and Ecclesiastes, for example—make no immediate sense at all. If a book's name seems strange, it's probably because the name is an English form of an ancient name. (See pages 179-230 for a summary of each book and an explanation of the names.)

Note that a few books contain numerals in the titles. In the Old Testament you'll find, for example, 1 and 2 Samuel. When you speak of these out loud, you say "First and Second Samuel," not "One and Two Samuel." The same applies to 1 and 2 Kings and to 1 and 2 Timothy, and to all other books with numerals in their names.

A note about the books by John. The New Testament has a large and important book called the Gospel of John. It is usually called John for short (as in "Our Bible study group is studying John for the next few weeks"). But the New Testament also has three epistles or letters written by the same John. These three are 1 John, 2 John, and 3 John. They are much shorter than the Gospel of John. If you see "John" without a number preceding it, the reference is to the Gospel of John.

What Are These Two "Testaments"?

The Bible's 66 books are divided into two parts. The first part, the Old Testament, deals with the beginnings of the world and of God's dealings with the people known as the Israelites or Hebrews. The New Testament, written later, deals with Jesus, his disciples, and the earliest groups of Christians. *Testament* means "covenant" or "agreement," and it refers to God's "contract" with his special people—the Hebrews in the Old Testament, the Christians in the new. You could think of *testament* as meaning "instruction manual" or "terms of agreement" for the people who wanted to know and do God's will.

What's in the Bible?

This instruction manual is, fortunately, more readable than most manuals. Unlike manuals, the Bible isn't written in a businesslike style. Within the 66 books are history (seldom boring), moral rules, rules about worship, advice for daily living, songs of praise and thanksgiving and despair, warnings against moral decay, prophecies, sermons, and more. With 66 books and many different authors, this kind of variety is to be expected.

Speaking of authors, the writers are a mixed group. Two of them, Moses and Paul, were well-educated by the standards of their times. But the other authors were (just to pick a few examples) fishermen (Peter, John), a tax collector (Matthew), a shepherd (Amos), kings (David, Solomon), a priest (Ezra), and a servant (Nehemiah). Not one of them was a "professional writer" in our sense of the term. Their written words were produced over a span of 1600 years. Given this time span, the 66 books, and the dozens of different writers, the Bible is obviously more than just a book. It is (and has often been called) the Book of books.

Unfortunately, all this diversity can be puzzling to a first-time reader of the Bible. Where should one begin? At page 1? Is it all worth reading, or are there parts that can be skipped? Which parts are really, *really* important? This book will try to answer all those questions, and more.

Why Is It Called "Holy"?

First, though, let's consider the Bible's other name: *Scripture.* This just means "writings," and when people talk about the holy Bible and the holy Scriptures, what they mean is "these writings are so honored and respected and so different from other writings that we consider them *holy* or *sacred.*" That is, they exist not just because human beings wrote them and passed them on through the centuries, but because they really were

> The Christian feels that the tooth of time gnaws all books but the Bible. It has a pertinent relevance to every age.
>
> W.E. SANGSTER

a revealing of God to humanity. Because people have considered the Bible holy, they have thought of it as something more than just pleasure reading or a historical curiosity. If people hadn't sincerely believed this for centuries, the Bible probably wouldn't still be around today, unless perhaps some archaeologists happened to dig up some ancient pieces of papyrus.

Consider the great epic poems *The Iliad* and *The Odyssey.* Both were written long ago, in roughly the same time period as certain books of the Bible. People still read these poems (both in the original Greek and in translated form) and discuss them. They are classics, as the Bible is. But no one *believes* in the truth of these poems. They may contain some historical material. But they are a mixture (a beautiful and well-written mixture) of mythology, religious beliefs, folk tales, and details about life in an ancient civilization—and they really don't have any bearing on how we live our lives and find meaning. But the authors of those poems knew they were just writing poetry. They never included the words "Thus says the Lord..."—a phrase that crops up again and again in the Bible. So there are old books such as *The Iliad* that are classics but not holy. The Bible, for people who accept it, is a "holy classic."

Is the Bible the Only Holy Book in Existence?

Christianity is not the only religion with scriptures or holy books. Most of the great world religions have some writings that they consider special. The fact is, all religions have traditions and teachings that are important. In what we call the "primitive" religions, these traditions may not be written down. The people of these religions may pass them on by word of mouth from one generation to another. Like the Bible, these traditions may include history, rules, and poetry.

The Jews have the Bible minus the New Testament, which they don't accept. Devout Jews order their lives around their Bible, particularly the first five books, which are known as the *Torah*. Many still follow the kosher food laws in the book of Leviticus (against eating pork, for example). Jewish rabbis and scholars have written hundreds of volumes of commentary on the Old Testament, so it is definitely a holy book for them.

The Muslims have the Qur'an (or Koran), written (unlike the Bible) by only one author, the prophet Muhammad. Muslims call it "the Noble Qur'an" or sometimes just "the Book." Muslims believe that *Allah*—God—was the ultimate source of the Qur'an. This book guides the lives of devout Muslims, and the society and culture of

DON'T APPROACH THE BIBLE AS A BOOK OF RULES

Well, the Bible *does* have rules. All religions do. So do all schools, employers, sports teams, any kind of human grouping. No one joins a baseball team and gripes, "I don't like this 'three strikes and you're out' rule." That's just baseball. Well, the Bible's assumption is that life, like baseball, has rules. They're not meant to stifle and repress. The rules are there for a good reason. (Any married person who's ever been suspicious of his spouse understands the wisdom of the "Do not commit adultery" rule. And anyone who owns any type of property understands "Do not steal." The rules aren't all bad, are they?)

But it is wrong to see the Bible as a book of "do nots." It has so much more: images of loving fellowship with God and with other people. The "do nots" are balanced with a lot of very positive "dos."

Muslim nations across North Africa, the Middle East, and elsewhere show the reverence people have for this volume.

Christians, Jews, and Muslims are "people of the book." In theory, these three religions' beliefs are supposed to be based on their holy books and on nothing else. Tradition, of course, also plays a role in their beliefs, but, in the final analysis, their books are the cornerstone of their beliefs.

Other religions also have holy books, but those religions don't have the same level of reverence for those books as Christians, Jews, and Muslims do for theirs. Confucianism, for example, is based on the teachings (and writings) of the Chinese teacher Confucius. But some people aren't sure whether Confucianism is a religion or just a philosophy. Confucianists respect Confucius' writings, but they don't really regard them as sacred.

The Hindu religion of India, which is very, very old, has many books—the Bhagavad-Gita, the Vedas, the Upanishads, and many others. Hinduism is more like a group of religions rather than just one, and there is no one book that the Hindus honor in the same way that Christians approach the Bible.

The Bible's view of humans' relationship with God is unique in all the world religions. In the Bible, God is the mighty King of the universe, the Master of all things, the awesome Supreme Being, the all-seeing Judge who knows our every thought and deed. Other religions have gods like this. But the Bible shows us other sides of this mighty God. He is approachable, he loves people, and he wants to be loved by us freely and willingly. He is not just the King, but also a father to those who love him. He wants his followers to be not only worshippers, but his *children*. As the Holy Spirit, this very personal God actually lives within his people, guiding and strengthening them. So the God of the Bible is uniquely both "Master of the universe" and "up close and personal."

Why Are There So Many Versions of the Bible?

Every bookstore in every mall sells Bibles—and more than one version, too. You can't buy the "real" Bible because the "real" one was written in ancient Hebrew and Greek. So we have to trust translators who know these languages to give us an accurate idea of what the original authors meant to communicate. Because languages change over time, no translation can be "permanent," although the King James Version, published in 1611, is still being read today. Words and phrases change, so every few years translation committees or publishers decide it's time for a "new and improved" translation of the old Book. There are literally dozens of English translations today, though a handful qualify as the most popular.

If you look inside the front of a Bible, you will usually find a preface or introduction. This will usually explain when and why the specific translation was done. Most people today find it easiest to read a translation done after 1970. And as time passes, new translations will have to be done.

There is no "official" version that everyone agrees is the best. The one quoted in this book is the New International Version, completed in 1978. It has been well-received by readers (one test of its value as a translation) and by scholars (the other test of its value). Some other popular versions are the New Revised Standard Version, the New Jerusalem Bible, the New King James Version, and Today's English Version (also called the Good News Bible). You'll often see these versions referred to by their acronyms—NIV for New International Version, for example, and KJV for (you guessed it) the King James Version.

What Do the Numbers in the Text Represent?

If you open your Bible to the first book, Genesis, you'll see a large "1" at the beginning, which indicates chapter 1. Back in the Middle Ages, the entire Bible was divided into chapters. Like the chapter divisions in any book, the chapters in the Bible help to break up the text and make it easier to locate a specific section. The smaller numbers in the text refer to verses. Generally there are one or two sentences in each verse, but not always. (The word *verse* does not mean that the material is poetry, by the way.) The verse divisions were done in the 1500s—again, to make it easier to locate a specific section. If you're looking for the Ten Commandments, it's much easier if someone tells you, "They're in Exodus chapter 20" instead of, "They're somewhere in Exodus." Usually, to be brief, you would simply say, "Exodus 20."

Before the Bible was divided into chapters (around the year 1214) and verses (in 1551), people had to refer to parts of the Bible by the name of the book or by the author (or whoever people thought the author was). People would refer to the book of Isaiah by saying, "As Isaiah says...," Or they would say, "As Solomon says in Proverbs...." The chapter and verse numbers are a tremendous help, as they allow readers to find the exact location of specific words in a particular book.

The one book in the Bible that isn't divided into chapters is Psalms. It consists of 150 separate poems, and these are referred to as psalms, never as chapters. They are, like chapters, divided into verses. Instead of saying "Psalms, chapter 23, verse 2," you would say, "Psalm 23, verse 2."

You will *never* find any book or speaker that refers to page numbers in the Bible. Instead, when you want to take people to a specific place in the Bible, you refer to the book, the chapter, and the verse. For example, a pastor will announce on Sunday, "I will preach this morning on John 3:16." This means his sermon will be about John (a book of the New Testament) chapter 3, verse 16. Note that a colon (:) always separates the chapter number from the verse number. Romans 12:1 means "Romans chapter 12, verse 1." A few books of the Bible have only one chapter, so they have only verse numbers. So Jude 14 means "Jude, verse 14."

The numbers are always the same for specific chapters and verses regardless of which Bible translation you use. In other words, no matter what Bible you turn to, you will always find at Exodus 20:14 words similar to "You shall not commit adultery."

What Are the Subheads in the Books?

Most Bibles have, in addition to chapter and verse numbers, sub-heads. For example, the New International Version has, in chapter

2 of Genesis, the subhead "Adam and Eve." These subheads aren't actually part of the Bible text. They are aids the translators insert to give you an idea of what a particular section is about. They serve the same purpose as chapter titles and subheads in a regular book. These are useful if you're looking for a particular subject, or if you're just browsing. For example, if you're looking for the Christmas story in Luke's Gospel, it helps when you find the heading "The Birth of Jesus" at the beginning of chapter 2 in Luke.

What Is the Apocrypha?

Some Bibles don't contain the Apocrypha, and others do. The books in the Apocrypha are an addition to the standard 66 books of the Old and New Testaments. All of the apocryphal books were written in—and most are concerned with—the long gap of time between the Old and New Testaments. When the Protestant churches broke away from the Catholic church in the 1500s, they questioned the Apocrypha, believing it wasn't "inspired" in the same way that the other books of the Bible are. Protestant leaders noted that the Jews' sacred books did not include the Apocrypha. All Catholic Bibles still include the Apocrypha. But the books of the Apocrypha have never been studied as closely or been considered as important as the other 66 books. We will deal more with the Apocrypha in a later section.

What Are *Text* and *Passage?*

When people speak of a portion or section of the Bible, they often refer to it as a *passage.* Example: "My favorite passage in the Bible is the parable of the good Samaritan in Luke 10." A passage is always more than one verse; it may be as long as a chapter, or even longer. *Passage* could mean the same as *verses,* except that *verses* can also refer to verses from different places in the Bible. A passage, however, always refers to a continuous set of verses.

Text is just a way of referring to the words. You could speak of "translating the Hebrew text into English." *Text* can also mean the same as *passage.* You might hear a pastor begin a sermon by saying,

"The text for my sermon today is Exodus 20:1-2." Or, someone might say, "The author quoted a Bible text in his novel," or "The author quoted a Bible passage in his novel." Both statements mean the same.

Why Are the 66 Books in a Specific Order?

First, the New Testament follows the Old (naturally). Second, there is a chronological sequence in both Testaments—sort of. The Old Testament begins, appropriately, with Genesis and its story of the world's creation. From Genesis to the book of Esther, the Old Testament books progress forward in time. But Esther is followed by Job, a book with no specific date attached to it. And Job is followed by Psalms, a collection of poems written over hundreds of years. Beginning with the book of Isaiah, the books known (collectively) as the Prophets fall into (roughly) a chronological sequence. Malachi, the last book of the Old Testament, is generally supposed to have been the last prophet before the "silent years" between the Old and New Testaments.

Why did the Old Testament not use a strict chronological approach? Some of the books—Psalms, Proverbs, and Ecclesiastes, for example—simply don't fit into a historical sequence. Over time, they found their niche between the historical writings (from Genesis to Esther) and the prophets (Isaiah to Malachi).

The New Testament begins with the birth of Jesus (told in the Gospel of Matthew), then gives the other three Gospels (Mark, Luke, and John), which are other accounts of Jesus' life. The Gospels are followed by the book of Acts, which tells the story of Jesus' followers after he had departed from the earth. Acts is followed by the epistles, or letters, written

> The Bible was never intended to be a book for scholars and specialists only. From the very beginning it was intended to be everybody's book, and that is what it continues to be.
>
> F.F. Bruce

to churches or individuals concerned with issues confronted by the early Christians. These letters aren't arranged historically. They are generally arranged according to size—that is, the first letter, Romans, is the longest. After the letters comes the last book, Revelation. It is the logical end to the Bible because it is concerned with the end of the world and the beginning of an entirely new world—heaven, that is. As in a good novel, Revelation is the climax, the "ending with a real bang."

If you are new to the Bible, there are two ways to get to know the location of the books: You can memorize the sequence of the 66 books, or you can get in the habit of looking at your Bible's alphabetical list of the 66 books in the table of contents, which will enable you to find the book by page number. (By the way, one Bible version of the 1980s, the Alphabetical Bible, arranged the 66 books in alphabetical order. This version didn't sell well at all.)

These are the names of the books of the Bible, along with the usual abbreviations:

Old Testament

Genesis	Gen.	Proverbs	Pr.
Exodus	Ex.	Ecclesiastes	Eccl.
Leviticus	Lev.	Song of Solomon	S. of S.
Numbers	Num.	Isaiah	Isa.
Deuteronomy	Deut.	Jeremiah	Jer.
Joshua	Josh.	Lamentations	Lam.
Judges	Jdg.	Ezekiel	Ezek.
Ruth	Ruth	Daniel	Dan.
1 Samuel	1 Sam.	Hosea	Hos.
2 Samuel	2 Sam.	Joel	Joel
1 Kings	1 Kgs.	Amos	Amos
2 Kings	2 Kgs.	Obadiah	Obad.
1 Chronicles	1 Chr.	Jonah	Jon.
2 Chronicles	2 Chr.	Micah	Mic.
Ezra	Ezra	Nahum	Nah.
Nehemiah	Neh.	Habakkuk	Hab.
Esther	Est.	Zephaniah	Zeph.
Job	Job	Haggai	Hag.
Psalms	Ps.	Zechariah	Zech.
		Malachi	Mal.

New Testament

Matthew	Matt.		1 Timothy	1 Tim.
Mark	Mark (or Mk.)		2 Timothy	2 Tim.
Luke	Luke (or Lk.)		Titus	Tit.
John	John (or Jn.)		Philemon	Phm.
Acts	Acts		Hebrews	Heb.
Romans	Rom.		James	Jam.
1 Corinthians	1 Cor.		1 Peter	1 Pet.
2 Corinthians	2 Cor.		2 Peter	2 Pet.
Galatians	Gal.		1 John	1 Jn.
Ephesians	Eph.		2 John	2 Jn.
Philippians	Phil.		3 John	3 Jn.
Colossians	Col.		Jude	Jude
1 Thessalonians	1 Thess. (or 1 Th.)		Revelation	Rev.
2 Thessalonians	2 Thess. (or 2 Th.)			

Why Are There Maps?

You don't need a map to enjoy or understand the Bible. But the Old and New Testaments both refer to events that took place in actual locations—cities, countries, rivers, etc. Since much of the Bible is history, maps are helpful, just as maps are helpful in any history book. Most Bibles contain at least a few maps that show the key places in the Old Testament (Israel and the nations that surrounded and conquered it) and the New Testament (Israel in Jesus' time, often with place names that have changed from the Old Testament names).

Why Are There Tables of Weights and Measures?

Back in Bible times, people did not use the same measurement systems we use today to refer to weights and measures. Nor was their money the same as ours. Most Bibles have charts or tables that show the rough modern equivalents of weights, measures, and money. A good modern translation of the Bible will probably communicate these things in the text itself.

What Is This *Concordance* at the End?

Some Bibles include a concordance, which is a sort of index. It lists the verses in the Bible that mention a particular word or name. Most

Bibles don't contain a *complete* concordance, which lists every word in the Bible and every verse that has that word. A complete concordance is large enough to require a whole book by itself. The concordances found in the backs of Bibles just mention certain selected verses and words. For example, a Bible concordance might list the word *love* and would cite such well-known verses as John 3:16 and 1 Corinthians 13:2. Many concordances are available today in a software format.

Why Is There a Dictionary at the End?

Your Bible may not have one, but it's a nice thing to have. What you have is really a mini-dictionary. Since the Bible is so big and contains so much information about people, places, and events, a comprehensive Bible dictionary is a full book all by itself. The dictionaries in Bibles usually list only the most important people, places, and things, giving a brief definition of each one and telling why it is important and where you can locate it in the Bible. This is a useful tool for new readers. For example, many parts of the New Testament refer to a man named Abraham, whose story is in the *Old* Testament. Your Bible's mini-dictionary may explain where you can find the story of Abraham (it's in Genesis, chapters 12 through 25) and why he is considered so important in both the Old and New Testaments.

Why Are There Footnotes?

You will notice that most Bibles have footnotes at the bottoms of the pages. Like footnotes in any book, these contain important information. And as with any book, the important thing is the book's text, not its footnotes. But the Bible is an old book, and many of the footnotes help explain information that might otherwise puzzle the reader. *Study Bibles* are Bibles with extensive notes. If your Bible is a study Bible, it will probably say so on the cover and the spine of the book (*NIV Study Bible, Life Application Study Bible, Oxford Study Bible* are just a few examples.) With a study Bible you get a lot of historical and theological information in the footnotes, usually written by well-respected Bible scholars. These notes explain such matters as dates of events, key ideas being expressed, and so forth. Some notes in study Bibles also explain how the passage applies to life.

Even Bibles that aren't study Bibles will sometimes have footnotes. Let's consider some examples from the New International Version's version of the book of Psalms.

At the end of Psalm 3, the Hebrew word *Selah* appears. The footnote at the page bottom says, "A word of uncertain meaning, occurring frequently in the Psalms; possibly a musical term." You don't have to know this to appreciate Psalm 3, but at least the footnote keeps you from puzzling over just what *Selah* means. (In effect, the footnote says, "Don't worry; the scholars aren't sure what it means, either.")

The same way, in Psalm 51, verse 6, you read, "Surely you desire truth in the inner parts." The accompanying footnote says, "The meaning of the Hebrew for this phrase is uncertain." (Good translators are humble enough to admit they don't know everything.)

Psalm 14, verse 1, contains the word *fool*. The footnote at the page bottom states, "The Hebrew words rendered *fool* in Psalms denote one who is morally deficient." The footnote is explaining that the Hebrew word doesn't translate exactly into any one English word. Our English word *fool* is close, but it doesn't quite convey that it has a moral as well as mental meaning.

Psalm 18, verse 2, describes God as "my shield and the horn of my salvation." *Horn*, you say? The footnote says, "*Horn* here symbolizes strength." The footnote is bridging a gap and translating a psalm many hundreds of years old, explaining that "horn" has a symbolic and not a literal meaning. (The people in Bible times, being closer to nature, generally thought of "horn" as "a thing on an animal's head," not "a musical instrument.")

Psalm 87, verse 4, says, "I will record Rahab and Babylon among those who acknowledge me." The footnote says that "Rahab" is "a poetic name for Egypt." Here is a case where the translation in the text itself is inadequate for clarity. The reader has heard of Egypt, but only a Bible scholar would know that "Rahab" and "Egypt" are the same. So the footnote supplies that bit of information.

Several places in Psalms the phrase "praise the LORD" occurs, always with this footnote: "Hebrew *Hallelu Yah*." In other words, our English "praise the Lord" is translating the Hebrew *Hallelu Yah.*

Psalm 136, verse 13, refers to "him who divided the Red Sea asunder." It is referring to the famous parting of the Red Sea in the book of Exodus (famous also in the movie *The Ten Commandments*). The footnote says, "Hebrew *Yam Suph;* that is, Sea of Reeds." The footnote is telling us, "Yes, 'Red Sea' is the name you probably know that sea by, but the actual Hebrew name means 'Sea of Reeds.'" A footnote like this lets the reader know that the translators are trying to be as accurate as possible.

Psalm 144, verse 14, reads, "Our oxen will draw heavy loads," and the footnote says, "Or *our chieftains will be firmly established.*" Here is a case of *alternate translation.* In many places in the Bible, especially with the Hebrew text in the Old Testament, more than one meaning (and more than one translation) could be right for a particular phrase. The scholars who made the translation put the most-likely-to-be-accurate translation in the text itself, but include the alternative in a footnote. In almost every case, the alternate translation is nothing that would change the meaning of the whole passage.

One classic example of a footnote giving an alternate translation is John 1:5. In the New International Version this verse reads, "The light shines in the darkness, but the darkness has not understood it." The footnote for the verse says, "Or *darkness, and the darkness has not overcome it.*" The experts on biblical Greek have yet to decide which is the more accurate translation. So the footnote lets you know there are two possible translations.

The Old Testament is quoted many times in the New Testament. In fact, almost any page in the New Testament will contain some quotation from the Old, since the New Testament authors comment on ways that Jesus fulfilled specific passages found in the Old Testament. In many cases a footnote will point out which Old Testament verse is being quoted. For example, Luke 22:37 reads, "It is written: 'And he was numbered with the transgressors.'" The footnote says, "Isaiah 53:12." If you choose, you can look up Isaiah 53:12 and read that verse in its original context. (This is similar to, for example, a teacher or author who states, "President Reagan once said...." If the Reagan quotation was followed by a footnote, it would tell you when and where Reagan made the remark.) Footnotes such as these are useful if you're curious about the Old Testament background of the New Testament.

This is called *cross-referencing*. It involves referring the reader to related Bible verses. Many of these point out where the New Testament quotes the Old Testament. Some also refer the reader to verses that cover the same ground. For example, some Bibles include a footnote for Matthew 5:3, the opening verse of Jesus' Beatitudes. The footnote might read: "Luke 6:20." This tells the reader that Luke 6:20 covers the same material.

In some cases you'll find a footnote in the New Testament that refers you to verses in both the Old and New Testaments. A classic example is Matthew 22:44, where Jesus quotes Psalm 110:1. The footnote for this might say, "Psalm 110:1." It might also add several other references: "Mark 12:36; Luke 20:43; Acts 2:35; Hebrews 1:13." These are other places where the New Testament quotes Psalm 110:1, and all the verses are related because they are referring to Jesus. By reading these verses, you could trace the way that Psalm 110:1 was interpreted by different New Testament authors. In many Bibles you would also find a footnote at Psalm 110:1 pointing you to the New Testament verses that quote it. So this kind of footnote allows you to "make connections" between various parts of the Bible.

By the way, footnotes in Bibles are not new. Since the invention of the printing press, most Bibles have contained notes explaining the text. Some old versions of the Bible had notes with a particular slant. For example, after Protestants split from the Catholic Church in the 1500s, there were Protestant Bibles with anti-Catholic footnotes and Catholic Bibles with anti-Protestant footnotes. A breakthrough came with the King James Version in 1611. Its translators had ruled that no notes could be added except for the explanation of the Hebrew or Greek texts. Happily, the vast majority of Bibles today aren't guilty of bashing other groups of Christians.

Why Do Some Bibles Include Words Printed in Red Letters?

Red-letter Bibles show the words of Jesus printed in red. Since Jesus is the key figure in the Bible, his words are more important than those of others, so some Bibles print his words in red to make them stand out from the rest of the text.

What Is Meant When People Say the Bible Is Inspired?

Harriet Beecher Stowe, who wrote the famous anti-slavery novel *Uncle Tom's Cabin,* claimed that "God wrote it." Did she mean that God actually wrote the novel and that she merely signed her name to it? Of course not. She meant that she wrote it, but that God's guidance was behind her writing of it. This is kind of similar to what people mean about the Bible being "inspired." The Bible did not just fall out of heaven, nor was it found written on golden plates. It was written section by section over a long period of time by many different writers. In any Bible translation—and particularly in the original Hebrew and Greek texts—you can't help but notice that the authors had different personalities. Paul's letter to the Romans has a very different style from the book of Acts, and the historical book of 1 Samuel is very different in style from the book of Ecclesiastes. Every author was different, just as present-day authors are different. God did not suppress or override each author's individual way of expressing himself as he penned the words of the Bible.

The idea that the Bible is inspired is more than just what Harriet Beecher Stowe talked about regarding *Uncle Tom's Cabin.* The Bible is said to be God's own words. An author can say he writes with "divine guidance" in the sense that he owes his life, intelligence, and way with words to God. But Christians believe that the Bible authors received *particular* guidance from God. This guidance kept the Bible free from errors. When we say the Bible is *inerrant,* this is what we mean. It is without error in that it is wholly true. That leads us to the next topic: historical authority.

SOME KEY STATISTICS ABOUT THE BIBLE:

The Bible has 66 books—
39 are in the Old Testament, and
27 are in the New Testament.

There are 1,189 chapters in the Bible, with
929 in the Old Testament and
260 in the New Testament.

There are 31,173 verses in the Bible, with
23,214 in the Old Testament and
7,959 in the New Testament.

The most common word in the English Bible is (surprise!) "and."

The longest *book* of the Bible is Psalms, with 150 chapters (actually, they're individual psalms, not chapters).

The longest *chapter* in the Bible (by far) is Psalm 119, with 176 verses.

The longest *verse* in the Bible is Esther 8:9—about 90 words long in most translations.

The shortest *verse* in the Bible has only two words: "Jesus wept" (John 11:35).

How Does the Bible Square with What Archaeologists Have Found?

Maybe a better question is, Can archaeology and other sciences prove the Bible is true? In a sense, no, because archaeology can't prove (or disprove) that God exists. Nor can it prove that God took a special interest in the Hebrews or Christians. What archaeology *can* do is confirm that the Bible's historical data is correct. In other words, archaeology can prove whether the Bible is recounting real history or just spinning a wild tale.

Back in the 1800s it became fashionable to believe that the Bible, particularly the Old Testament, was just folk tale and legend. For example, the Old Testament refers to a tribe of people called the Hittites, and no archaeologist up to that era had ever found evidence that the Hittites existed. Skeptics assumed the Hittites were just fiction—like the Wookiees in *Star Wars*. But—surprise!—in 1906 archaeologists working in Turkey found evidence that confirm almost everything the Bible says about the Hittites' customs and location. Also, from time to time archaeologists discover clay tablets and monuments bearing the names of people in the Bible. For example, Omri, a king of Israel (2 Kings 3) is mentioned on the Moabite Stone, which was cut in the ninth century B.C. Another king of Israel, Jehu (2 Kings 10), is mentioned on the Black Obelisk of the Assyrian king Shalmaneser III. An official inscription of Assyrian king Sennacherib mentions that he shut up the Judean king Hezekiah "like a bird in a cage"—exactly the words expressed in the Bible (2 Kings 18). The Babylonian Chronicle mentions that King Nebuchadnezzar conquered Jerusalem and imprisoned its king, Jehoiachin—exactly the story the Bible tells (2 Kings 24).

Genesis, the first book of the Bible, covers some very ancient times. Historians used to assume that Genesis' ancient stories of Abraham, Isaac, and Jacob were just fiction, written hundreds of years later and having no basis in reality. But archaeologists have found out a lot about those ancient times—family customs, travel, etc.—and they now believe that the early stories in Genesis reflect the times accurately.

Since the New Testament is much nearer to our own time, there is even more historical evidence available to us regarding this era. No one seriously doubts anymore that Jesus existed (although this was a trendy idea in the 1800s), and the various Jewish and Roman officials mentioned in the New Testament were all real, as confirmed by Roman inscriptions and records. In 1992, archaeologists found the family tomb of Caiaphas, the high priest who presided at the trial of Jesus. Like Caiaphas, Herod, Pontius Pilate, Felix, and other figures mentioned in the New Testament were real men, not just inventions of the Gospel writers.

These are just a few examples of archaeology supporting what the Bible says. As you might imagine, the further back in time you go, the less evidence there is. For instance, archaeologists leave no doubt in our minds that King David and King Solomon were real, historical characters. But, going back further, they find less evidence for Moses, even less for Abraham, and (naturally) none for Adam and Eve. That doesn't mean that these figures are fictional. It just means that evidence is harder to come by when you go further back in time. (If you've ever worked on your family's genealogy, you'll have run into this same problem. It's easy tracing down family members in the 1900s, less so in the 1800s, even less so in the 1700s, etc.) Archaeology cannot convince an unbeliever to believe in God. It can, however, provide a believer with evidence that the parts of the Bible claiming to be history really do have a foundation in fact.

When you begin to study the Bible, you'll notice that two important historical events are critical for belief: in the Old Testament this is the Israelites' miraculous exodus from Egypt, and in the New Testament it is the resurrection of Jesus from the dead. Archaeology has yet to prove—or disprove—either of these events. If Jesus was raised from the dead, then obviously no evidence could ever be produced. It is possible that further evidence could be found to support the Israelites' exodus, but no archaeologist could ever prove that it occurred because of God's miraculous intervention in making it happen. Archaeologists can't report on miracles, obviously. They can only report on inscriptions, official court records, and the other leftovers of civilization—coins, tombs, tools, etc.

Isn't the Old Testament Just a Confusing Hodgepodge of Laws and Strange Stories?

The Old Testament has no immediately apparent "plan" or plot in the way that a good novel or movie has. The only "plan" binding it all together is God's own plan of revelation. In a sense it *is* a hodgepodge—songs, poems, law, ritual, historical narrative, prophecy. The underlying theme that binds it all together is that God reveals himself to people and calls them to have a relationship with him and be faithful to him. It *does* take some sifting through the Old Testament to see this theme.

Readers often expect the Bible to be full of good role models. There are some of those, even in the Old Testament. But the Old Testament is pretty candid in portraying all the sins of human-kind—warts and all. Israel's heroes are not idealized storybook figures (which is one good reason to believe in the Bible's histor-ical accuracy). The heroes—people such as Abraham, David, and Solomon—show both good and bad sides. These were good, God-fearing men—but prone to deceit, violence, sexual promiscuity, and other vices. This is appropriate because for the Bible authors, God is the real hero of the story. Much as the Jews honored people like David, the Bible is consistent on one fact: God alone deserves the praise for everything good. (Consider the logic of this: Instead of telling us to worship all-too-human heroes with clay feet, the Bible says, "Worship God—even the best human beings can be failures at times.")

At the time Jesus appeared on the scene, many non-Jews, or Gentiles, had become admirers of the Jewish religion. In some cases they became full converts. Most of these people were attracted to the high moral standards in the Old Testament. They were not attracted by the Bible's "heroes," but by its ethics and its emphasis on a moral God. They also were not attracted to the Bible because of its literary value. Compared to the great writings of Greek and

Roman literature, there are portions of the Bible that are not considered great literature (a prime exception is the book of Psalms). The Bible's style was too blunt and straightforward compared with the writings of the Greek poets.

But many people believed that fine writing was not enough. In a time of moral breakdown, they yearned for a high morality, and they wanted to worship a God who urged them on to a better way of life. Many of them found this in the Jews' sacred book, the Old Testament. Just as in our own day, when many politicians and preachers urge a return to biblical standards of morality, so many people in the Roman Empire promoted the moral standards of the Old Testament.

Aren't Americans a Religious People Who Are Familiar with the Bible?

According to most polls, yes, Americans consider themselves religious. A majority say they believe in God, prayer, heaven, and hell. They even say these beliefs are "very important" to them.

But other polls show that people—even regular churchgoers—are very ignorant about what's in the Bible. Most people who respond to these polls cannot identify major characters and beliefs in the Bible, the Ten Commandments, the Beatitudes of Jesus, etc.

In short, polls show that Americans say they believe in God. But since many of them don't know the Bible (which is supposed to be our chief source of information about God), what exactly is their "God" like? A cosmic "force"? A Creator who is not really involved day-to-day in human life? Nature? The universe itself, us included? The average person's idea of God may be so vague that believing in God may mean believing in…nothing. Getting acquainted with God must involve (besides prayer, naturally) getting familiar with the Book, believed to be the Word of God himself.

WHY READ THE BIBLE?

Reason 1—Joy

We're so busy having fun in our culture that there's no time for joy. How often do you hear someone speak seriously about feeling *joy*? Along with Christianity itself, the concept of joy is definitely passé in both pop and high culture today. Yet it's an attractive idea, one that people in serious moments admit is missing from their lives.

Joy is *not* missing from the Bible. The popular image of people of faith is that they are long-faced, gloomy, and repressed. There are a few of these types around, but not in the Bible. In both the Old and New Testaments, the people of faith experienced joy in life—not the kind like a temporary emotional or chemical high, but something they could hold onto during the worst of times.

Can this still be had? Of course. The Bible is worth reading if only to find out just what the joyful people had, and why. (In case you're curious, the words *joy, joyful,* and *rejoice* occur over 300 times in the Bible.)

Reason 2—Values and Morals

You hear a lot today about family values and returning to traditional morals and religion for the good of society. The problem with all this talk from politicians and culture analysts is that people inevitably ask, "Why?" Then they follow with the logical question, "Do you expect me to be or act religious just for the sake of my kids and their kids? I can't do it if I don't believe the religious thing is actually *true*." In other words, why act Christian or semi-Christian if you aren't convinced that Christianity (based on the Bible) is true? The answer "It's good for you" doesn't wash. Faith is either alive or dead, absent or present.

So getting to know the Bible will resolve one question: Is this faith based on the Bible really true? Some people have studied the Bible and concluded, "No." Many others have said, "Yes, it is. So what it teaches about life and morals is important." Not many people have believed that the faith taught in the Bible was "sort of" important or moderately important. After studying the Bible closely, most people conclude that it is true and thus extremely important, or false and thus not important at all.

Reason 3—Critiquing the Church

The Bible has been called "the church's memory committed to writing." The history of Christianity throughout the centuries is, in essence, the story of how Christians have interpreted the Bible and attempted to be Jesus' followers. Some of the failures of so-called Christians are well-known, such as the medieval Inquisition, the bloody Crusades, etc. Every generation of Christians—ours included—fails in some ways to measure up to the standards set forth in the Bible. These failures are no reflection on the Bible itself. High standards are not a problem. Failing to meet them is the problem.

Unbelievers and believers both need to be familiar with the Bible, if only to be able to understand how Christianity does and does not square with its beliefs. When people criticize certain Christian practices, it's helpful to know if those practices are "real Christianity" (as the Bible sees it) or some sad misunderstanding of it. In other words, if you reject Christianity or certain aspects of it, at least be conscious of whether you're rejecting the real thing or some perversion of it. (An example: If you're offended by door-to-door evangelists, at least be aware the practice *is* vouched for in the Bible. On the other hand, if you're bothered that some of these evangelists try to pass off the Book of Mormon as sacred Scripture, this is *not* vouched for in the Bible.)

Reason 4—The Alternatives

A lot of people sneer at the Bible, its characters, its message. Consider some popular alternatives: *TV Guide, People, Vanity Fair, Penthouse, Golf Digest.* These stimulate…

1. the mind—not at all

2. the morals—not at all, or for worse

3. the imagination—a lot, but not necessarily in the best ways

Reading these magazines won't send you to hell. But they won't do you much good, either. Plus, they get stale *very* fast. A month-old issue of *People* is, well, boring. So at least consider the option of reading something that has been stimulating people's minds, morals, and imaginations for 2000-plus years. After that long, there must be *something* worthwhile in the Bible.

Reason 5—Understanding Culture

I love art museums, but like many museumgoers, I look at some of the modern artworks and, in puzzlement, say, "I just don't get it."

I don't have this same problem with the older paintings, the old masters. If you don't know the Bible well, you might have difficulty with older art. Many of the artworks before 1700 or so were pictures and sculptures of Bible scenes. Art museums across the world are filled with pictures of Jesus' birth, his crucifixion, the Last Supper, David killing Goliath, God creating Adam and Eve, Moses and the Ten Commandments, etc. You can admire these pictures and find them beautiful, but if you don't know the Bible, you might miss the point. The artists created these works for people who knew the stories. They weren't just being clever with a paintbrush. They were portraying scenes that people would immediately understand.

An example is a painting of the Last Supper. (There are hundreds of these, not just the famous one by Leonardo da Vinci.) If you know the Gospels, you know that Jesus and his 12 disciples had one final meal together before Jesus' crucifixion. In paintings of the Last Supper, one of the men is usually shown holding a bag in one hand. Who is he, and what is the bag all about? If you know the story, you know that Judas Iscariot was the disciple who betrayed Jesus for 30 pieces of silver. In the picture, Judas is usually shown with his money bag. A minor point? Maybe. But the more you know about the Bible, the more you can appreciate such artworks.

Think also about the world's great literature. The great novelists and poets frequently refer to ideas and characters from the Bible. Some writings, like John Milton's great poem *Paradise Lost,* are hard to grasp unless you have a basic knowledge of the Bible. Even William Shakespeare's works are full of references to people and events in the Bible. In more modern times, authors (even ones who don't consider themselves Christians) use biblical ideas and phrases. John Steinbeck gave two of his novels titles from the Bible: *East of Eden* and *To a God Unknown.* In both books he based modern characters on characters from the Bible. Another great author of the twentieth century, William Faulkner, gave biblical titles to his novels: *Absalom, Absalom,* and *Go Down, Moses,* for example. His novel *A Fable* is a modern retelling of the story of Christ.

The Bible isn't a dead book today. In 1996 the city of Richmond, Virginia, erected a large statue of tennis star Arthur Ashe, who had been born in the city. Engraved in huge letters on the pedestal is a long quotation from the letter to the Hebrews in the New Testament. Our culture may not be very Bible-literate anymore, but it's obvious that people still have a feeling of respect or maybe even affection for the Bible.

Can you be a well-read and knowledgeable person without knowing the Bible? You can, but you wouldn't have the same understanding and appreciation of some of the best that culture has to offer.

Reason 6—Find Out What the Media Aren't Telling You

We learn about our world by...what? Watching television, surfing the Internet, listening to the radio, reading newspapers and magazines, right? There's a problem, however. The media people, the people we rely on to inform us, often overlook things—sometimes deliberately. For example, did you know that some of the best-selling books in the last 30 years have been Christian books? And did you know that the best-selling nonfiction book of both 1972 and 1973 was a contemporary Bible version? (It was *The Living Bible,* by the way.) Writing in the *National Review,* David Scott noted that Christian authors "will never appear on the *Publishers*

Weekly or *New York Times* best-seller lists. Because of the way the bookstores surveyed for these lists are chosen, Christian books are segregated in a literary ghetto, although most of them are at least equal in literary merit to Danielle Steel and *The Bridges of Madison County*" (June 17, 1996, p. 50). The Bible and Christian books are big sellers, which means lots of people are reading them...maybe more people than you'd think. If these books are that popular, and if the media have some reason *not* to tell you how popular they are, shouldn't you find out why they sell so well? And shouldn't you find out why some would want to keep this a secret?

2

Papyrus, Scrolls, and All That:

HOW WE GOT THE BIBLE

W̶e take fax machines, copiers, and desktop publishing for granted. It's quite easy today to produce a letter, a brochure, or even an entire book in a small amount of time—produce it and *re*produce it. And we've had such capability for a very short time. On the great time line of world history, the mass production of written materials is a recent blip. The printing press, the first means of mass-producing books, didn't come along until the 1400s. Before that, written materials were reproduced through one method—the copycat method. A real flesh-and-blood human scribe had to copy a book (or scroll) word for word. Flip through the pages of your Bible (or a Stephen King novel, for that matter) and consider how long it would take you to copy every word of the book.

Why is it important to know this? Very simply, it means that in the pre-printing-press era (most of human history, that is), people didn't "dabble" at writing. Writing was laborious, publishing was laborious, and writing materials were usually expensive. Scratch pads and Post-it notes were not an option.

So when people wrote things down, they did so with a purpose. When archaeologists find written materials that are thousands of years old, they find mainly two things: sacred writings (like the Bible) and official writings (court records, for example). The average Joe (or Jo) in ancient times didn't keep a diary or dash off letters to friends every day. In fact, the average Joe probably couldn't read or write. He had to rely on professionals—scribes—to fill in the literacy gap.

All this means that the writings that got passed on generation to generation were pretty serious stuff. You wouldn't spend day after day carefully writing a copy of the book of Psalms unless you thought the book of Psalms was worth passing on. You wouldn't do this just to "preserve a slice of history," and you probably wouldn't do it because you thought the Psalms were "good reading." You would engage in this painful process because you honestly thought that your own generation, and the next, *needed to have the Psalms.* This is the only real explanation we can give for why the books of the Bible have been passed on for hundreds of years. Having considered the *why,* let's look at the *how.*

You Think Paper Grows on Trees?

The earliest forms of paper didn't. It grew on weeds. Specifically, it was made from a water plant, papyrus, which grows in Egypt and elsewhere. The ancient Egyptians discovered that papyrus stalks could be cut into strips and laid in crisscross fashion to form a flat, durable writing surface. (We get our word *paper* from *papyrus,* naturally.) In the dry climate of Egypt and other parts of the Middle East, pieces of papyrus have lasted for centuries—much longer than a page of modern-day wood-pulp paper would last.

Papyrus could take the form of pages, but for anything of great length—the book of Genesis, for example—long sheets of papyrus were put into the form of scrolls. In the Bible, when you find a reference to someone reading a *book,* mentally insert the word *scroll,* for that's the form in which literature was preserved in those days. Most contemporary Bible versions are accurate enough to use the word *scroll.* The writing on these scrolls appeared in columns on only one side. Scrolls did not have print on both sides, as do modern-day books.

Papyrus wasn't the only writing material available (though it had the advantage of being fairly cheap). Animal skins, leather in very thin form, could also be used for writing. (Recall that people used to refer to a diploma as a *sheepskin*.) Leather was a valuable commodity, and if it was written on, it could be recycled—the old writing scraped off and new writing put on. (History repeats itself. During America's Civil War, the South endured a paper shortage. So Southerners would recycle letters by turning the paper sideways and writing a new letter at right angles to the old one.)

When it came to making a scroll, sheets of papyrus were glued together, while leather pieces were stitched together.

The Hebrew Obsession with Detail

The ancient Hebrews/Israelites were a "people of the Book." They had great reverence for the books that we now call the Old Testament. Using their Hebrew alphabet (written right to left, by the way), they took great pains to copy and recopy the sacred books onto scrolls. Many stories have been told about how fanatical the copyists were about adding and deleting nothing in the copying process. Believing that the books really were the word of God, a copyist was denied the option of editing or polishing the words. These copyists were humble souls. No copies contain the names of the copyists or the date of their composition. But they were very good at what they did. Scholars are amazed that Hebrew scrolls made hundreds of years apart are almost exactly alike. The Jews were very careful about passing on the Old Testament as they received it.

So what became of the original scrolls—the ones actually written by Moses, Isaiah, Solomon, and others? Who knows? There is, in fact, no way of proving that a scroll could be an original. But we do have some old, old copies. The oldest ones found are now known as the Dead Sea Scrolls, discovered in 1947 in some caves. Scholars believe that among these scrolls are the oldest copies we have of the Old Testament books of the Bible. They date from roughly 250 B.C. to A.D. 65.

The Dead Sea Scrolls were written in Hebrew, the language of the Old Testament. Curiously, at the time these scrolls were copied, many Jews did not use Hebrew in the everyday situations of life. Jews were

EXPRESSIONS FOUND IN THE BIBLE

You may be quoting the Bible without even knowing it. Consider some everyday expressions from the King James Version, first published in 1611:

- Wolves in sheep's clothing: "Beware of false prophets, which come to you in sheep's clothing, but inwardly they are ravening wolves" (Matthew 7:15).

- Salt of the earth: "Ye are the salt of the earth" (Matthew 5:13).

- Drop in the bucket: "Behold, the nations are as a drop of a bucket" (Isaiah 40:15).

- Fat of the land: "I will give you the good of the land of Egypt, and ye shall eat the fat of the land" (Genesis 45:18).

- My brother's keeper: "The LORD said unto Cain, Where is Abel thy brother? And he said, I know not: Am I my brother's keeper?" (Genesis 4:9).

- Spare the rod and spoil the child: "He that spareth his rod hateth his son" (Proverbs 13:24).

- Giving up the ghost: "Man dieth, and wasteth away: yea, man giveth up the ghost, and where is he?" (Job 14:10).

- The skin of my teeth: "I am escaped with the skin of my teeth" (Job 19:20).

- Woe is me!: "Then said I, Woe is me! for I am undone" (Isaiah 6:5).

- Pride goes before a fall: "Pride goeth before destruction, and a haughty spirit before a fall" (Proverbs 16:18).

- Eat, drink, and be merry: "A man hath no better thing under the sun, than to eat, and to drink, and to be merry"

(Ecclesiastes 8:15), and: "Take thine ease, eat, drink, and be merry" (Luke 12:19).

- A lamb to the slaughter: "He is brought as a lamb to the slaughter" (Isaiah 53:7).

- Can a leopard change his spots?: "Can the Ethiopian change his skin, or the leopard his spots?" (Jeremiah 13:23).

- Holier than thou: "Come not near to me; for I am holier than thou" (Isaiah 65:5).

scattered across the Roman Empire, and though Hebrew was their "official" language, many of them spoke and read the common Greek that was the Roman Empire's unofficial international language. This Greek wasn't the same elegant literary Greek of classics such as *The Iliad* and *The Odyssey*. It was a sort of basic Greek used by ordinary people, including tradesmen and travelers. (Note: though the New Testament was written in Greek, the language spoken by Jesus and his disciples was Aramaic, a common language of the Middle East in those days. Occasionally you'll find places in the New Testament

IMAGINE ENGLISH WITHOUT AEIOU

A language without vowels? The Greek of the New Testament has vowels, but not the Hebrew in the Old Testament. Ancient Hebrew was consonants, and nothing more. So how did people know how to pronounce the words? The same way we do: habit. (We learn that *death* is pronounced DETH, not DEE-ATH, from *hearing* it pronounced this way, not by looking in a dictionary.) The Hebrews passed on their pronunciations by word of mouth.

But as Hebrew gradually ceased to be a common, spoken language, the copyists raised a logical question: Future generations will be able to read the sacred Hebrew books, but will they know where the vowel sounds are? In other words, if they read the Hebrew text out loud, how will they know how to pronounce these words without the vowels in place?

Along came the unsung heroes of Bible tradition: the Massoretes *(Massorah* is the Hebrew word for "tradition"). This is the group name of the scribes who inserted marks called "vowel points" into the Hebrew text. These points indicated, as far as they could tell, the accurate vowel sounds in the words. Working from the sixth century on, the Massoretes did us a tremendous service. The texts they have bequeathed to us are the basis of *Biblica Hebraica,* the standard Hebrew text that translators use today.

where one of the writers translates an Aramaic word. For example, in Mark 5:41, Jesus says the Aramaic words "*Talitha koum!*" and Mark translates it as "Little girl, I say to you, get up!" If you saw the 2004 film *The Passion of the Christ,* you might recall that the characters spoke in Aramaic.)

The New Testament was written in Greek. And, years earlier, so was the Old Testament translation known as the Septuagint. Completed in Egypt (which had a large Jewish community), the Septuagint became *the* Old Testament for the many Jews who no longer understood the original Hebrew.

The Septuagint is significant for several reasons. One is, being in Greek, it made the religion of the Hebrews "exportable." Greek was spoken and read in Rome, Egypt, North Africa, even as far away as Spain. Because the Old Testament was available in Greek, it could be read by people across the Roman Empire. This is why many non-Jews became admirers of the Jews' religion. For those already familiar with the Old Testament, the foundation for Christianity had been laid. Many non-Jews who read the Old Testament and had come to expect a Messiah, or Christ, were well prepared to hear the message of Christianity.

Greek continued for many years as the international language, so the Septuagint was copied and recopied. So were the Gospels, letters, and other writings of the New Testament—all in common Greek. Bible scholars and archaeologists like to comb through ancient digs to find scrolls—or even tiny scraps of scrolls—to see just how ancient a Bible passage they can find. Some have been found that are 100 years or less after those books were originally written, which is remarkable.

In addition to papyrus scraps, archaeologists have also found *codices*—plural for *codex.* A codex was not a scroll but a book, with text on both sides of the pages, and the pages stitched together at the edges. Like scrolls, they were copied by hand. The importance of the codices is that they "put it all together"—that is, they show the New Testament being published as a unit. The oldest codices are Codex Vaticanus and Codex Sinaiticus, both from about the mid-300s A.D. (Interestingly, these ancient books lay buried until the 1800s.)

Take a Yawn Break and ask the obvious question: Why is this history lesson important? The simple answer is that we ought to have a Bible as close as possible to the original manuscripts. Since we can't have the originals (if they even exist now), we ought to try to find

CANYOUREADTHIS

Would you care to read a New Testament passage as it was delivered to its original readers? Here's Matthew 5:3-5, citing the English words instead of the original Greek:

BLESSEDARETHEPOORINSPIRITFORTHEIRSISTHEKINGDOMOFHEAV ENBLESSEDARETHOSEWHOMOURNFORTHEYWILLBECOMFORTED BLESSEDARETHEMEEKFORTHEYWILLINHERITTHEEARTH.

Did you have any trouble following that? This is what the New Testament Greek text looked like—no punctuation, no spaces between words, no lowercase letters. The text was comprised of just one long string of letters (all capitals), one after another.

So how could people read such material? To put it mildly, Greek is very different from English. In Greek, words change form based on the role they play in a sentence. Our word "cat" is always "cat," changing only when we adds an "s" to indicate a plural or an "'s" for a possessive. But a Greek noun would change form depending on whether it was the sentence's object or subject, plural or singular. It could also change to indicate the presence of a preposition. What the Greeks lacked in punctuation marks, spaces, and lowercase letters they made up for in a rich variety of words.

Something else was missing: paragraphs. Your Bible is divided into paragraphs—and probably into sections with subheads that indicate the subject matter of that particular block of text. (You might see a subhead that reads "The Beatitudes" over Matthew 5:3, for example.) These help the reader to know where a specific section begins and ends.

the oldest copies. Logically, the older the Greek and Hebrew copies are, the closer they are to being like the originals. Let's be honest here: Copyists tried hard to copy these texts precisely. But to err is human, and so changes crept into the copies. Once a change or error crept in, there was a good chance it would be copied and recopied. According to those who have researched these ancient copies, none of the changes are truly significant. (You won't find a copy that says Jesus was *not* the Son of God, for example.) But the many, many copies that have been unearthed do show differences—*variants*, the scholars call them. Most of the changes involve spelling variations or minor sentences or phrases added into the text.

For these reasons, the ideal that modern-day translators strive for is to produce a Bible based on the oldest manuscripts. The other important test is not just how old the manuscripts are, but how much agreement is found between them. This is a matter of majority rule: If one manuscript shows a variation not found in hundreds of others, the scholars tend to side with the majority. After all, that one odd variation might have been caused by a drowsy copyist—or one trying to "improve" the text or add his own opinion.

This, in short, is why Bible translators show such a passion for studying Greek and Hebrew—and for digging up dusty old scraps of papyrus. And modern translators are fortunate—they have more ancient manuscripts available to them than any other translators in history.

An important reminder about errors in the text of the Bible: The key teachings of the Bible are found all throughout its pages, not in just a few isolated passages. In spite of many minor variations among the old Greek and Hebrew manuscripts, none of the Bible's important teachings have been affected in any way. What the Bible teaches about God, creation, man, sin, salvation, Jesus, the Holy Spirit, heaven and hell, and morals has not been affected by the minor variants found in the old manuscripts.

From Greek to Latin to...

While Greek was still commonly spoken during the first three centuries after Christ's death, there eventually came a need for the Bible to be in Latin, too. But the earliest attempts at this showed mixed results. From A.D. 366 to 385, a man named Damasus was the bishop of Rome, and he wanted to make a solid translation of the Bible into Latin.

Damasus's secretary was a workaholic scholar by the name of Eusebius Hieronymus Sophronius—thankfully, also known more simply as Jerome. Trained in Latin and Greek classics, Jerome had also studied Hebrew. (Hebrew is a difficult language to learn, requiring intense study and concentration. Jerome believed that studying Hebrew kept his mind busy and free from sinful thoughts.) By the time he entered Damasus's service, Jerome was an outstanding scholar of the Bible.

Damasus asked Jerome to produce a new Latin translation of the Bible, one that would throw out the inaccuracies of earlier Latin translations. Jerome began in A.D. 382. After 23 years of labor, he finished his translation in 405. (If 23 years seems like a long time for a translation, consider that Jerome was working alone. Also, this workaholic scholar was churning out volumes of Bible commentaries and other writings during these years.)

At first Jerome worked from the Greek Old Testament, the Septuagint. But then he established a precedent for all good translators: the

THE MATERIAL CHURCH'S CRITIC

Jerome is best known as the great translator and creator of the Latin Vulgate Bible. But Jerome was a busy bee, somehow finding time to write on almost every subject of the times. He frequently played the role of Christian critic, scolding the church for being too materialistic. In Jerome's view, a wealthy church with lavish buildings was a far cry from the simple Christianity of the New Testament. According to Jerome, "Our walls glitter with gold, and gold gleams upon our ceilings and our pillars. Yet Christ—in the form of the naked, hungry, and poor—is dying at our doors."

Old Testament would have to be translated from the original Hebrew. In his quest for accuracy, Jerome consulted many Jewish rabbis. He referred to the Old Testament in its original language as *Hebraica veritas*—Latin for "Hebrew truth."

While translating the Old Testament, something struck Jerome: The books the Jews regarded as holy Scripture did not include the books we know as the Apocrypha. So Jerome did not wish to include them in his translation. However, they had been included in the Septuagint, the basis of most older Latin translations, and Jerome was compelled by the Roman Church authorities to include them. But he made it clear that, in his opinion, the Apocrypha was only *liber ecclesiastici* ("church books"), not quite like the fully inspired *liber canonici,* the "canonical books"). The books of the Apocrypha could, he said, be read for enrichment, but not for establishing Christian doctrine. Hundreds of years later, the leaders of the Protestant Reformation would follow Jerome's advice and either not include them in Protestant Bibles, or place them in a separate section. Due to Jerome's influence, Catholic and Protestant Bibles differ to this day. (Jerome was not always consistent with himself. In some of his writings he quoted from books of the Apocrypha and referred to them as sacred Scripture.)

"The Divine Library," as Jerome called the Bible, was finally available in a well-written, reasonably accurate translation in the language commonly used in the churches of Western Europe. Jerome had enormous clout as a scholar, and his translation became the standard. Known as the *Vulgate* (from the Latin word *vulgus,* meaning "common"), it was later used as the basis for translations of the Bible into other languages.

This had some good and bad effects. On the good side, the Vulgate was a pretty reliable translation. It was highly regarded by all scholars in the Middle Ages. Indeed, Martin Luther, though he knew Hebrew and Greek, quoted Jerome's Vulgate throughout his life. (When Luther translated the Bible into German, however, he used the Greek and Hebrew originals—just as Jerome had done.)

On the bad side, Jerome was a tough act to follow as a translator.

His cherished translation had the Roman Church's seal of approval, and this put a damper on new translations being made from Hebrew and Greek. Not for a thousand years did scholars again attempt translating from the Greek New Testament.

So why didn't some sensible soul say, "Hey, let's gather together the Greek and Hebrew books of the Bible and translate them into our own language"? Actually, some people did. But the church authorities, who had become powerful people as time passed, frowned on this. They were afraid of what might happen if the average farmer or baker or merchant had access to the Bible. It might cause...what? Revolution? Perhaps what the church authorities feared was losing their position as the official interpreters of the Bible. So long as the Bible was in Latin, it was a book for a privileged class, the "brain elite." Besides, the common folk didn't need to read the Bible for themselves, since the church authorities would tell them all they needed to know about faith.

So the Bible became, in effect, a closed book. Scholars who knew Latin discussed the Scriptures and wrote commentaries—in Latin. In theory, their knowledge would trickle down, via the parish priests, to the people. Did this happen? Not too well. By the 1400s the church had gone a long way from the churches in the book of Acts, churches where new believers tested preachers' sermons against the Scriptures. Many ministers led lives of scandalous immorality, which was easy enough, since most people were fairly ignorant of the Bible's moral teachings.

The situation changed with the two overlapping movements we call the Renaissance and the Reformation. Both movements urged "getting back to basics," and the Reformation leaders went further and insisted that the Bible be available in the common people's languages—English, German, Spanish, whatever. Latin was dead, and the Bible was supposed to be a living document.

Technologically, the timing was perfect. Something amazing had been sprung on the world: the printing press.

The Gutenberg World

In the 1440s, in the German city of Mainz, a goldsmith named Johann Gutenberg was experimenting with movable pieces of metal type. This, he reasoned, might be a means for mass-producing books and getting around the toil of copying them by hand.

In 1456 Gutenberg—or a group he was a part of—printed a book: the Bible. Specifically, it was the Latin translation by Jerome, the *Vulgate.* Though this translation was now very old, the printing of it started a revolution that would affect people who had no knowledge of Latin.

First, a word about the Gutenberg Bible's appearance: It was stunning—it was a work of art that has never been equaled in the history of printing. Some book collectors say that the first printed book is also the most beautiful printed book ever. Gutenberg's typeface resembled the beautiful handwritten letters the scribes had used for ages (called *Gothic,* or *black-letter*). Later, in the interest

CHAPTER AND VERSE

The chapter divisions in the Bible weren't part of the original Hebrew and Greek writings. They were introduced around the year 1214 by Stephen Langton, who became archbishop of Canterbury (England's chief clergyman). Langton's chapter divisions were adopted not only by the Christian church but by Jews also. Langton didn't have to divide the book of Psalms into chapters because the book was already divided into 150 separate psalms. The shortest books (such as Obadiah, Philemon, and Jude) he did not divide at all.

The verse divisions in the Bible didn't appear until 1551. Robert Estienne, a French scholar and printer, was responsible for the work. According to his son, he did the work while riding on horseback across France. (Some people believe that this jerky form of transportation explains why some of the verse divisions appear in odd places.)

In Mainz, Germany, you can visit the Gutenberg Museum and see not only a Gutenberg Bible but also a replica of Gutenberg's print shop. Looking at the massive mechanisms used in the world's first printing job, it's easy to imagine that Gutenberg (or his assistants) must have moonlighted as bodybuilders or bouncers. Not only was the world's first printed Bible extremely bulky, but so was the press it was printed on. (By the way, Gutenberg's real first name was Gensfleisch. The poor man was not fortunate in the matter of names.)

of economy, more straightforward, less artsy typefaces developed that were easier to read and easier to cast in metal. (Incidentally, Gutenberg's Bible had no title page nor page numbers. It would take a while before anyone thought of including page numbers in books.)

Here was a revolution: Books could be mass-produced so that more people could have access to them. The Bible could be available in large quantities—not only in scholarly Latin, but also in translations people could understand. Martin Luther realized this and translated the Bible into a readable German version that was used for centuries.

A major thrust of the Reformation was the desire of people to return to biblical faith and practice. Such a reform might have been impossible in the pre-Gutenberg age. An inaccessible Latin Bible would cause no major shake-up. Indeed, many Catholics argued that God *meant* for the Bible to be kept from the people's hands. (In fact, the official position was that the Latin translation was an inspired text, just as the original Hebrew and Greek texts had been inspired.) Only the theologians, the Catholic authorities said, could interpret it properly. (Obviously there was some intellectual snobbery at work here.) Luther and other Reformers said no—give the Scriptures to every plowboy and serving-maid. The Bible and the believer together are enough. No priest, no pope, no official church council needs to stand between a person and the Word of God. Everything the Reformers said about the priesthood of all believers was rooted in the assumption that people could have access to the Bible in their own language. It was appropriate, then, that in one of the books Gutenberg printed, he stated that "the Highest reveals to the humble what He conceals from the wise."

As Bibles and other books were printed, a cycle began: More people became readers, and these readers demanded more books. Even for the illiterate the Bible was accessible because at least a literate pastor could read from, and preach about, a Bible that could be understood. And most households had at least one literate person who could read aloud to the rest of the family. The idea that every person should be able to read was rooted in the idea that every person should know the Bible.

This new access to the Bible made ordinary men and women feel a part of the dramatic world of the Bible. Religion among Protestants did not end at the church door; thanks to the mass production of Bibles, every household could become a training ground for faith. As the Reformers wished, the boundary between pastor and layman was breaking down. A home could, with the Bible in hand, legislate its own morals. At one time people asked, What will I have to confess to the priest? But now they could ask, Is my life in line with the Bible?

It is hard for us to fathom the significance of this revolution. The Bible is so very accessible to us these days—even on a portable computer or on the Internet. But imagine how awesome it was to a sixteenth-century layman to have the words of the Lord spoken in his native tongue. We may never know such a feeling—the feeling that at long last God's Word could be spoken to us directly, and that our own eyes could read and ears could hear God's Word firsthand.

The Bible in English

Wherever the Protestant Reformation spread, Bible translations were made. The most famous was the German version done by the great Martin Luther himself. Closer to our own culture, King Henry VIII of England (famous for having six wives) had broken from the Catholic Church, but he still prohibited any Bibles in

HOW THE ENGLISH LANGUAGE
HAS CHANGED OVER SIX CENTURIES

That the English language has changed a lot over the last few centuries becomes very evident when we look at the change in the wording of Psalm 23:1-4 in different English Bibles.

- *Wycliffe version, 1384*
  The Lord governeth me, and no thing to me shal lacke; in the place os leswwe where he me ful sette. Ouer watir of fulfilling he nurshide me; my soule he convertide. He brogte doun me upon the sties of rigtwisnesse; for his name.

- *Coverdale Bible, 1535*
  The LORDE is my shepherde, I can wante nothinge. He fedeth me in a grene pasture, and ledeth me to a fresh water. He quickeneth my soule, & bringeth me forth in the waye of rightuousnes for his names sake.

- *King James Version, 1611*
  The LORD is my shepherd; I shall not want. He maketh me to lie down in green pastures: he leadeth me beside the still waters. He restoreth my soul: he leadeth me in the paths of righteousness for his name's sake.

- *Today's English Version, 1976*
  The LORD is my shepherd; I have everything I need. He lets me rest in fields of green grass and leads me to quiet pools of fresh water. He gives me new strength. He guides me in the right paths, as he has promised.

- *New Living Translation, 1996*
  The LORD is my shepherd; I have everything I need. He lets me rest in green meadows; he leads me beside peaceful streams. He renews my strength. He guides me along right paths, bringing honor to his name.

English. Translator William Tyndale had to do his English translation in Europe and have it smuggled into England, where the church bishops burned all copies that they found. (Consider the irony: the bishops, the spiritual heads of the church, ordering the Word of God burned!) Then, later, Henry got the Protestant bug and decreed that every English church should possess the Bible in English.

Within 100 years of Henry's decree, more than one English Bible appeared. Before we consider those, let's backpedal a few centuries. Though the Catholic Church had outlawed translations, they were done anyway. Before the outlawing was official, some interesting translations of the Bible had been made. Caedmon, a simple farm boy, had done some free translations of parts of the Bible into Anglo-Saxon (Old English, the same language as the old epic poem *Beowulf*). Some priests had translated the Psalms into Anglo-Saxon, also. The beloved King Alfred the Great is supposed to have done some translating into Anglo-Saxon before he died in 901. But the most notable name associated with the English Bible is John Wycliffe, a kind of pre-Protestant Protestant—that is, he believed the Bible (not the pope or the church bureaucracy) was the sole authority for Christians. Wycliffe, a pastor and scholar with some

FAMOUS FIRSTS: THE GENEVA BIBLE

The Geneva Bible, an English translation published in 1560, broke some new ground. It was the first Bible to be divided into verses as well as chapters. It was the first to use standard roman type, not the ornate (and hard-to-read) Old English type. And it was the first English Bible to be read widely in homes. Part of this was due to its size—is was a lap-sized Bible as opposed to a large pulpit-sized Bible. Until the King James Version of 1611, it was the "people's version"—the version William Shakespeare would have read, and the version the Pilgrims brought to America on the *Mayflower*. The Geneva Bible was also the official version of the Church of Scotland.

aristocrat friends who protected him from being arrested by the church authorities, published an English Bible sometime around 1385. (The actual translating was done by some of Wycliffe's associates, but for convenience's sake, this is usually called the Wycliffe version.) The translation was done from a Latin text, since practically no one in England at that time could have translated the Bible from the original Hebrew and Greek. (By this period, the early 1400s, English was in the form we call Middle English—the language of Geoffrey Chaucer's *Canterbury Tales*.) The church showed its opinion of Wycliffe's work: Years after his death, a church council ordered his body dug up and burned.

Wycliffe's version circulated in manuscript form for 150 years. The church authorities in England decreed that reading an English Bible was a criminal offense. People read it anyway. Because copies were so rare and expensive, people were willing to pay a "rental fee" to study a copy of the Bible for an hour or so. Some common folk such as farmers would pay for this privilege with produce. With so many people being illiterate, nonreaders would gather around while some brave soul read to them the Bible in their own language. (The next time you see your Bible sitting on a shelf gathering dust, remember that 600 years ago, a poor man might pay a load of hay just for the privilege of reading the Bible for an hour.)

Now, back to the 1500s. The earliest official (meaning *legal*) English version was the Great Bible, basically a revision of Tyndale's and Coverdale's translation, and officially authorized by King Henry VIII in 1539. In St. Paul's church in London, six copies were set up, and crowds gathered to hear the Bible being read in…English. It's hard for us to appreciate the shock and novelty of this. The Bible in our own language—heavens! Readers—and illiterate people who wanted to hear the Bible being read aloud—came in droves. Some illiterates, including older adults, learned to read just so they could read the Bible for themselves.

The Great Bible, true to its name, was a "pulpit Bible"—bulky and expensive. The next great innovation was the Geneva Bible, printed in clear Roman type rather than ornate Old English type. It

"I'M HENRY THE EIGHTH, I AM..."

In the history of the English Bible, King Henry VIII is both hero and villain. King Henry split the Church of England from the Roman Catholic Church in the 1500s. Such splits were taking place elsewhere in Europe, and the new churches were called Protestant. But Henry didn't see himself, or England's church, as Protestant. He still considered himself a good Catholic, but a Catholic without a pope. So while the Protestant churches in Germany and elsewhere were abandoning the Latin Bible and producing translations in their own national languages, Henry said, "Not in my country you don't." Henry was afraid that enabling the people read the Bible in English might lead them to come up with all sorts of revolutionary ideas. The Catholic leaders had been saying the same thing for centuries.

William Tyndale labored to make an English translation—the first English Bible to be produced on a printing press. In the new age of the press, Bibles could be mass-produced. But Tyndale had to work in another country because Henry VIII decreed that Tyndale's English Bible must be "clerely extermynated and exiled out of the realme of Englande for ever." Even so, courageous souls managed to smuggle the new translation into the country. Tyndale translated the entire New Testament and a large portion of the Old. Sadly, the Catholic emperor Charles V had Tyndale arrested and burned as a heretic before he completed his Old Testament.

In the meantime, King Henry had joined up with Europe's Protestants—for political, not religious, reasons. To show them that he had really broken free from the Roman Catholic fold, he did a Protestant thing: He ordered that a translation of the Bible be made into his national language. The new English Bible was—surprise!—the Tyndale version, completed by Tyndale's friend, Miles Coverdale. The new and officially legal English Bible was completed in 1535 and dedicated to King Henry VIII. So Henry, who had at one time prohibited Bibles in English, was the first English king to have a Bible dedicated to him.

was smaller, more portable, more suited to home use. First printed in 1560, it became England's "family Bible" for many years. You might say that the Geneva Bible was the first "household book" in the English language. If a family could afford to own only one book, it was the Geneva Bible.

The Amazing KJV

"To the most high and mighty Prince, James, by the Grace of God…" So begins the dedication at the front of the most popular English Bible of all time, the Authorized Version, better known as the King James Version. The much-loved KJV (as it is often abbreviated) has lost popularity in recent years as more readable modern translations have become available to twenty-first-century readers. But generation after generation of English and Americans have absorbed its phrases. It is doubtful that any other version will ever have such an effect on the English language.

Who was the "mighty Prince, James" whose name has been stamped on millions of Bibles? He was the son of the colorful ruler Mary Queen of Scots, who was executed by England's Queen Elizabeth I. Ironically, when the childless Elizabeth died, James was her successor, since he was the next male in the royal line. Already king in his native Scotland, James marched south to London to be crowned king of England, too.

Under Elizabeth, the Church of England had assumed a definite form: It was not Catholic—that is, it did not bow to the pope, and certain elements of the Catholic mass had been discarded. But it wasn't as noticeably Protestant as the Lutheran and Calvinist churches in Europe. Many people felt that Elizabeth had created a "compromise" church that wasn't Protestant enough. Known as Puritans, these people wanted to "purify" the church of anything that resembled Catholicism, including bishops, priestly garb, and too much ritual.

The Puritans hoped that James would push the English church in the right direction. After all, he had been raised in the very Protestant country of Scotland. Before the new king even reached London, they presented him with the Millenary Petition, so-called because it had a thousand signatures. These signatories asked for changes in the Church of England. James surprised them. He rather liked the Church of England with its pomp and ritual. In fact, he told the Puritans they must "conform themselves" or he would "harry them out of the land."

But the Puritans were a large group, and James couldn't push them aside so easily. In January 1604, a conference of church leaders met at the royal palace at Hampton Court, near London. On the whole, the conference was a failure for the Puritans—except on one point: James gave his approval to creating a new version of the Bible. He was aware that the Bishops' Bible, the official version published during the reign of Queen Elizabeth, had never been popular with the people. The Geneva Bible of 1560 was popular, but James didn't like it, even though it had been the official Bible of his native Scotland. An exceptionally vain man, James must have liked the idea of having England's official Bible associated with his name.

James appointed 54 scholars for the creation of this new translation. They were divided into companies of seven or eight men each, working both individually and in conference. Then the whole text was gone over by a committee of 12. While the scholars consulted the original Hebrew and Greek texts, they also leaned on other subsequent translations. In fact, the KJV is not really a translation—it is a revision of earlier versions. In a long preface to the new version, the scholars admitted that their work was not a totally new translation but a "new and improved" version of older translations. (If you know someone who is a "King James only" person, you might remind him of this.) The work of William Tyndale, the first major English translator, is evident in many passages, and so is the wording of the popular Geneva Bible (which leaned on Tyndale). We should be glad that the revisers chose to retain some of the fine wording of the older versions as well as creating some fine phrases of their own.

Work began in 1607 (the same year the English colony of Jamestown was established in America), and the new Bible was published in

LOOKING FOR A CATCHY
TITLE FOR A BOOK?

Any author knows that you can't just write a good book. You have to give it a good title to help it sell. In the past, and even in the present, authors have found the Bible to be a great source of book titles. And inevitably the version they choose from is the old reliable of 1611, the King James Version.

- American novelist John Steinbeck's *East of Eden*

  "And Cain went out from the presence of the LORD, and dwelt in the land of Nod, on the east of Eden" (Genesis 4:16).

- American novelist Ernest Hemingway's *The Sun Also Rises*

  "The sun also ariseth, and the sun goeth down, and hasteth to his place where he arose" (Ecclesiastes 1:5).

- American novelist William Faulkner's *Absalom, Absalom*

  "The king [David] was much moved, and went up to the chamber over the gate, and wept: and as he went, thus he said, O my son Absalom, my son, my son Absalom! would God I had died for thee, O Absalom, my son, my son!" (2 Samuel 18:33).

- Ben Ames Williams's 1947 Civil War novel *A House Divided*

  "When the Pharisees heard it, they said, This fellow doth not cast out devils, but by Beelzebub the prince of the devils. And Jesus knew their thoughts, and said unto them, Every kingdom divided against itself is brought to desolation; and every city or house divided against itself shall not stand" (Matthew 12:24-25).

- English poet Robert Browning's collection *Bells and Pomegranates*

  The title is from a description of the Israelite high priest's robe: "Beneath upon the hem of it thou shalt make pomegranates of blue, and of purple, and of scarlet, round about the hem thereof; and bells of gold between them round about: A golden bell and a pomegranate, a golden bell and a pomegranate, upon the hem of the robe round about" (Exodus 28:33).

- American novelist Winston Churchill's *The Inside of the Cup*

  "Woe unto you, scribes and Pharisees, hypocrites! for ye make clean the outside of the cup and of the platter, but within they are full of extortion and excess" (Matthew 23:25). (By the way, this isn't the same Winston Churchill who was England's prime minister.)

- French novelist Marcel Proust's *Cities of the Plain*

  "Abram dwelled in the land of Canaan, and Lot dwelled in the cities of the plain, and pitched his tent toward Sodom" (Genesis 13:12). The "cities of the plain" are the immoral Sodom and Gomorrah, which are destroyed by God. Proust's original French title was *Sodome et Gomorrhe*.

- American novelist Edith Wharton's *The Valley of Decision*

  "Multitudes, multitudes in the valley of decision: for the day of the LORD is near in the valley of decision" (Joel 3:14).

> "Those who talk of the Bible as a 'monument of English prose' are admiring it as a monument over the grave of Christianity."
>
> AMERICAN-BORN POET
> T.S. ELIOT, 1965

1611. From that time on it has been called the Authorized Version in England.

Officially, the new version was "appointed to be read in churches," replacing the Bishops' Bible. But it was a long time before it replaced the Geneva Bible as the Bible of individual readers, particularly the Puritans. James, who died in 1625, did not live to see the KJV achieve wide acceptance. But once it was established, it was unshakable. Even though some critics said that its language was already outdated in the year it appeared, later generations loved its "Bible English." As the English language evolved, becoming less and less like the language of King James's day, English-speaking Christians continued to express themselves in terms echoing the KJV. (To name but one example, multitudes of Christians still address God as "Thee" and "Thou.")

And how the language has been affected! Even if the KJV were to someday go out of print—which is unlikely—our language still bulges with such immortal expressions as "the skin of my teeth," "Woe is me!" "a drop in the bucket," "my brother's keeper," "holier than thou," "thorn in my side," "wit's end," "apple of my eye," and many others.

But the effect goes beyond phrases. There is a cadence, a sentence rhythm, in the KJV that has never been matched in subsequent English Bibles. It's true that the obvious beauty of the KJV's words has probably discouraged some readers from truly hearing the message. But the KJV, born in the age of Shakespeare and other brilliant authors, couldn't help but be incredibly *memorable* and *memorizable*. If learning Scripture is important, then committing it to memory is important, and we know that poetry, or poetic prose, is easier to memorize than flat prose. Here in the twenty-first century, most people who can quote the Bible inevitably quote the version published in 1611.

From King James to Today

What has happened to the Bible between the release of the King James Version in 1611 and our own time? A lot. We now have far greater numbers of very early manuscripts, including those found among the Dead Sea Scrolls. So today we have a better idea than the King James translators of what the original Bible was like.

Why all this fuss about finding the oldest manuscripts? Consider an analogy: Let's say your great-grandfather left a handwritten will many years ago, something that interests you for historical purposes. What would you trust more: the original will, or a copy of a copy of a copy of that will? If you can't get the original, you would at least want the oldest copy. True, the differences in all the copies might be very minor. But you would want to get as close as possible to the original. This is exactly the aim of Bible scholars.

So the new finds in ancient manuscripts—plus the fact that people no longer speak "King James English"—has required updated translations into English. The King James Version of Mark 10:14 has Jesus saying, "Suffer the little children to come unto me, and forbid them not." The New International Version reads, "Let the little children come to me, and do not hinder them." Which is clearer? The King James Version used "suffer" in a way we no longer use it. Changes in language have required newer translations for clarity's sake.

There was, and still is, to some degree, some resistance to contemporary translations. The affection people had for the KJV has proved very strong. But people need to remember that the King James Version itself was a "new and improved update" in its own time (1611). The KJV translators were aware that the English language had "outgrown" the older versions—just like a growing child can't keep wearing the same clothes.

People say they love the language of the King James Version. It is still impressive. And no wonder—it was written in the same era that produced William Shakespeare and other great authors. But the original Greek and Hebrew texts of the Bible were in everyday vocabulary. They weren't written in an artsy or classy way for highbrows. They were not written in the language of literary classics. They communicated in very direct, basic words. And when the King James Version was published in 1611, it was in the very direct, basic English of the day. But 400 years later, that language is no longer everyday English. People say the KJV is dignified and solemn and majestic. It does seem that way. But for every reader who likes (and understands) the ornate language of the KJV, there are many other readers who can't grasp the language. The old-fashioned English makes the Bible seem distant, too "holy" to be read—or maybe just plain irrelevant in the modern world

Another shortcoming of the older versions: They often reproduced the long, cumbersome sentences of the original Hebrew and Greek texts. So, while the translations were often accurate, they were written in sentences that modern readers find hard to swallow at times. Today, people prefer bite-sized words and sentences.

One additional deficiency of older versions such as the King James is a deficiency in ourselves, actually. Modern readers are no longer familiar with theological terms that were fairly well-known in times past. For example, the King James rendering of 1 John 2:2 says that Jesus is the "propitiation for our sins." How many people do you know who can define *propitiation?* (Can *you* define it?) One modern version, the Jerusalem Bible, does much better with "the sacrifice that takes our sins away." Today's English Version has "the means by which our sins are forgiven." That's clearer, don't you think?

But people liked the King James Version so much that at first, translators hesitated. "Why not," they asked, "just revise the KJV, updating the language in places, and correcting it where necessary?" This was exactly how new versions were done in the 1800s and early 1900s. The popular Revised Standard Version (RSV) of 1957 was this type of version. All these revisions, by the way, added something noticeably missing from the KJV: quotation marks. This made it much easier to tell who was speaking to whom. (Some later editions of the KJV have added quotation marks.) Most of these versions also eliminated the old "thees" and "thous."

In the 1960s and 1970s something new happened: Translators

began to make new translations based on the original Hebrew and Greek texts and bypass the KJV entirely. One was the 1970 New English Bible, which has been more popular in Britain than in the United States. Another was the simple and straightforward Today's English Version (TEV, also called the Good News Bible). Published by the American Bible Society in 1976, the TEV impressed people with its simplicity. In 1971 Kenneth N. Taylor released *The Living Bible*, which went on to become a phenomenal best-seller. Readers loved it, but highbrows snubbed it because, as Taylor admitted, it was a paraphrase (a rewording, that is) of the English version, not a translation from the Greek and Hebrew.

One interesting version that some people like is The Amplified Bible. Its name has nothing to do with sound or speakers, but with the interesting way that words are added [in brackets, like these] to help show the meaning of the text. This looks a bit odd [peculiar, unique] when you first read it, but once you get used to the bracketed words, you'll find they serve the purpose of making the original Greek and Hebrew meanings clearer. (Don't try reading it aloud in a church service, however.)

Two readable contemporary versions for Catholics are the New Jerusalem Bible and the New American Bible (sometimes sold in stores as The Catholic Bible). These two versions include the books of the Apocrypha. Both these versions were translated directly from the original Hebrew and Greek texts, breaking with the longtime Catholic tradition of translating from the Latin Vulgate.

One very popular translation—the one generally quoted here in this book—is the New International Version, or NIV, published in 1978. It continues to be the most popular version among evangelical Christians. The New Living Translation (NLT) is also popular among evangelicals. Evangelicals who like the "feel" of the KJV but want more clarity can go to the English Standard Version (ESV) or the New King James Version (NKJV), both of which continue the tradition of updating the language of the KJV.

In the 1980s and 1990s, some publishers produced what are called "gender-inclusive" versions. These—the New Revised Standard

(1989), the Revised English Bible (1989), and others—aim to eliminate language that some people consider sexist. For example, they use *humanity* or *humankind* instead of the older generic term *man*. Some readers like this. Others feel that it leads to some clumsy wording or even obscures the meanings in the original texts. (The obvious advantage of the word *man* is that it can refer to one individual as well as to the entire human race. This is also true of the Greek word *anthropos,* which translators have accurately translated as *man*. However, the words *humanity* and *humankind* cannot refer to just one individual.)

Which version is the "best" Bible in English? The obvious answer is, *the one you actually read.* Most people—especially those who are very new to the Bible—do best with a good contemporary translation such as the New International Version or the New Living Translation. One other factor to keep in mind as you make your choice: If you're going to be involved in a church or Bible study class, it makes sense to get the version that most other members of that group use because it helps when everyone is "on the same page." This may mean owning two versions of the Bible (one for personal reading, and the other for group settings), and that can be good, because sometimes comparing versions helps to bring more clarity to the text you're reading.

Accuracy, or Clarity?

Sentences in the original Hebrew and Greek texts were often very long and complex. Older English translations of the Bible were faithful to the original languages to the extent that they not only translated the words (and ideas) but also the sentence structure. So the translations were accurate, but often difficult to read.

As an example, consider the first sentence in the letter to the Hebrews. Here's how it reads (very accurately) in the King James Version:

> God, who at sundry times and in divers manners spake in time past unto the fathers by the prophets, hath in

these last days spoken unto us by his Son, whom he hath appointed heir of all things, by whom also he made the worlds; who being the brightness of his glory, and the express image of his person, and upholding all things by the word of his power, when he had by himself purged our sins, sat down on the right hand of the Majesty on high (Hebrews 1:1-3).

Whew! Now, that is a *long* sentence—one that very accurately reflects the words of the original Greek text. But all those commas and clauses…mercy! Maybe we contemporary readers have a bad case of Attention Deficit Disorder, but it's just hard for us to read a sentence that long—accurate or not. (If you ever read the novel *Moby Dick,* you've had some exposure to some *really* long sentences.) Compare the wording in Today's English Version:

In the past God spoke to our ancestors many times and in many ways through the prophets, but in these last days he has spoken to us through his Son. He is the one through whom God created the universe, the one whom God has chosen to possess all things at the end. He reflects the brightness of God's glory and is the exact likeness of God's own being, sustaining the universe with his powerful word. After achieving forgiveness for the sins of mankind, he sat down in heaven at the right hand of God, the Supreme Power.

The modern version actually runs a little longer than the King James. But it is broken down into three sentences, while the KJV is all one sentence. Yet all the thoughts are there in both versions. Technically, the King James is closer to the original Greek text.

But which is easier to read? You choose.

THE BIBLE IN AMERICA: SOME CHOICE TIDBITS

1492 and the Bible

Christopher Columbus came to America guided by...the book of Isaiah. Columbus, a devout believer, claimed that his voyage across the Atlantic fulfilled a prophecy of Isaiah: "From a far-off land, [I summon] a man to fulfill my purpose. What I have said, that will I bring about; what I have planned, that will I do" (Isaiah 46:11).

After his third voyage to the New World, Columbus wrote *A Book of Prophecies*. In it he explained how his voyages had fulfilled numerous prophecies in the Bible. He was absolutely certain that "neither reason nor mathematics aided me. Rather, the prophecy of Isaiah was completely fulfilled."

The first Bible printed in America was not in English but in the Algonquin Indian language. During the colonial era, all English Bibles had to be printed in England.

The Bible and American Leaders

President Thomas Jefferson produced his own version of the Gospels. He cut out all the miracles and had the Gospels end with Jesus' burial, not the resurrection.

Abraham Lincoln's second inaugural address, given in 1865, quotes from the Bible twice. Here are the words from Lincoln's speech: "It may seem strange that any men should dare to ask a just God's assistance in wringing their bread from the sweat of other men's faces, but let us judge not, that we be not judged." The words Lincoln used from the Bible are as follows:

"In the sweat of thy face shalt thou eat bread" (Genesis 3:19 KJV).

"Judge not, that ye be not judged" (Matthew 7:1 KJV).

Abraham Lincoln's speech at the 1858 Republican convention in Springfield, Illinois, included one of Lincoln's most-quoted lines:

"A house divided against itself cannot stand." (Lincoln was refer-ring to the North-South division occurring in the country.) Lincoln borrowed his line from the Bible, Matthew 12:25: "Every kingdom divided against itself is brought to desolation; and every city or house divided against itself shall not stand" (KJV).

John F. Kennedy's 1961 inaugural address contains a quote—or near-quote—from Luke's Gospel. Kennedy said, "For of those to whom much is given, much is required." Here's the verse from Luke 12:48: "For unto whomsoever much is given, of him shall be much required" (KJV).

Franklin D. Roosevelt's 1933 inaugural address contains these words: "The money changers have fled from the high seats in the temple of our civilization." Consider Matthew 21:12-13: "Jesus entered the temple area and drove out all who were buying and selling there. He overturned the tables of the money changers and the benches of those selling doves" (NIV).

The great American statesman Daniel Webster gave a speech in 1831 in which he praised Secretary of the Treasury Alexander Hamilton. In the speech Webster said, "He smote the rock of the national resources and abundant streams of revenue gushed forth. He touched the dead corpse of Public Credit, and it sprung upon its feet."

Consider these two Old Testament passages: "Moses lifted up his hand, and with his rod he smote the rock twice: and the water came out abundantly" (Numbers 20:11). "It came to pass, as they were burying a man, that, behold, they spied a band of men; and they cast the man into the sepulcher of Elisha: and when the man was let down, and touched the bones of Elisha, he revived, and stood up on his feet" (2 Kings 13:21).

Patrick Henry, a leader of the American Revolution, often quoted or alluded to the Bible in his great speeches. In a 1775 speech at the Virginia convention, Henry said, "The battle, sir, is not to the strong alone." Ecclesiastes 9:11 says, "I returned, and saw under the sun, that the race is not to the swift, nor the battle to the strong." In the same speech Henry said, "The gentlemen may cry, Peace, peace! but there is no peace." And Jeremiah 6:14 says, "They have healed also the hurt of the daughter of my people slightly, saying, Peace, peace; when there is no peace."

Ach!

The first American Bible in a European language was not in English. In 1743 Christopher Sauer of Pennsylvania published an edition of Martin Luther's German Bible. German Bibles did not fall under the British colonial law that said all English Bibles had to be printed in England.

Cherry Trees and Bibles

Mason Weems, who concocted the tale of young George Washington chopping down a cherry tree, made a living as a Bible salesman. Around 1800 he wrote to his publisher, "This is the very season and age of the Bible. Bible dictionaries, Bible tales, Bible stories, Bibles plain or paraphrased—so wide is the crater of public appetite at this time!"

Noah Webster, father of the American dictionary, published an "Americanized" King James Version in 1833. His version dropped British spellings and eliminated the old-fashioned wording of the KJV. This was a time period when Americans were trying hard to prove they were distinct from their former masters, the British. Webster's version did not sell well, but in the twentieth century, almost all his changes were incorporated into modern translations.

Reed the Bye-bul?

The strangest spellings in a Bible must be those in Andrew Comstock's Filadelfia New Testament, published in 1848. Comstock concocted a "purfekt alfabet" so readers would know exactly how to pronounce every word.

The first book printed in America was not the Bible, but almost was. It was the *Bay Psalm Book,* a rhyming version of the Psalms, published in the 1600s in Massachusetts.

Julia E. Smith of Connecticut was the first woman to translate the entire Bible all by herself. Her translation was published in 1876.

The Hare family of Philadelphia published the *Christian Spiritual Bible* in 1881. It differed from other Bibles in one notable way: it taught reincarnation, a belief that had some popularity in the 1880s (as well as in our own day...).

Lew Wallace, a Union general in America's Civil War, set out to write a book proving that Christianity and the Bible were false. The more he studied, the more convinced he became that the Bible was true. Instead of writing an anti-Christian book, he ended up writing the novel *Ben-Hur*, which also became one of the most popular movies of all time. The novel's subtitle is *A Tale of the Christ.*

Best-sellers?

In the years 1953-54, the best-selling nonfiction book in the United States was the new Revised Standard Version of the Bible. In 1961 it was The New English Bible: New Testament. In both 1972 and 1973 it was *The Living Bible.* Oddly, best-seller lists in those years did not even mention these books. Why? Because most best-seller lists—such as those in the *New York Times*—did not list religious books. Beginning in the 1990s, best-seller lists became more correct (and more honest) by including religious best-sellers.

3

The Authority Problem:

INSPIRATION, INERRANCY, AND INFALLIBILITY

Singer Bob Dylan had a hit with "You Gotta Serve Somebody." The song was about a pretty simple idea: Each of us bows to some authority. We stake our lives on someone—or something—that we consider reliable, dependable.

True, sometimes we claim to be self-reliant, looking no further than ourselves for guidance. But the bookstore shelves are full of books of advice. So are the airwaves, with their multitude of radio call-in "experts." (Odd that the books and radio hosts talk about *self*-help, isn't it? The fact that you're reading the book or calling the radio host means you want someone else's help.) And the Internet is full of self-appointed "experts." The most self-reliant people around would, if they were honest, admit they aren't totally self-reliant. They will, at least in some areas of life, bow to someone else's authority.

What Do You Think of the Bible?

Your attitude toward the Bible is a measure of how you see its authority—or lack of it. If you see the Bible as just a human document, a collection of fiction and people's harebrained religious ideas, then you won't see the Bible as having any authority at all. It may be interesting, but not authoritative. You might even admit that it has a few good insights into human nature. But you'll probably say that, as a whole, it's just an interesting book with no real importance for human life today. This is the same view many readers today have of classic Greek poems such as *The Iliad* and *The Odyssey*—interesting, with some good insights into human life, but not really relevant for building our lives around.

At the other end of the spectrum is the person who believes the Bible is inspired. It is the word—the *ultimate* word—of God to man. It contains everything we need to know about our destiny as human beings in this world and afterward. It is able to meet our deepest needs.

Between these two extremes are different shades of opinion. When ten people say, "I believe in the Bible," they may mean ten very different things. (When you hear about recent polls that show that most Americans have positive feelings about the Bible, don't assume that their "belief" in it is all too clear.)

Let's consider the source of the Bible's authority: God. The Bible is not supposed to be authoritative in itself. Like any book, it is ink on white paper. But it is authoritative because it represents the ultimate authority, God. Jesus made this sort of claim. He acted, according to witnesses, with authority. But he claimed that the real authority was his Father, God: "The words I say to you are not just my own. Rather, it is the Father, living in me, who is doing his work" (John 14:10). (From here onward, to save from confusion, all texts quoted from the Bible are in the New International Version unless otherwise noted.) Yet people believed that God had delegated power and authority to Jesus: "All the people were amazed and said to each other, 'What is this teaching? With authority and power he gives orders to evil spirits and they come out!'" (Luke 4:36).

The prophets of the Old Testament didn't claim to speak or act on their authority. They claimed to speak for God. The phrase "This is what the Lord says…" (or "Thus says the Lord…" in some versions) is spoken again and again by the prophets. But Jesus never used that expression. He claimed to receive his authority from God, but unlike the prophets, he never said, "This is what the Lord says…" He spoke with *his own* authority—as if his words and God's words were the same. This is what the first Christians believed: that Jesus was, in some way beyond our understanding, God. His authority is God's authority. "I and the Father are one" (John 10:30).

No one has ever claimed that Jesus wrote the Bible. He didn't. But the New Testament is *about* Jesus. It claims to present, accurately, what he said and did. It claims to present what his earliest followers believed about him. They must have believed very strongly, because quite a few of them paid the ultimate price for their belief.

The Bible does not say much about its own authority. Why would it? Would you ask a fortune-teller or an astrologer or a psychologist, "Are you for real?" Of course not. A document might contain the words "Read me; I am inspired and authoritative." But what kind of witness is that? Wouldn't a fake document make the same claim? The Bible has four Gospels. There were plenty of other Gospels that didn't make it into the Bible. Many of these actually claimed to be the "real" story of the "real" Jesus. One of the fake Gospels was even called the Gospel of Truth. Few people read these anymore, except as historical curiosities. They're full of otherwise unsubstantiated stories about Jesus working miracles in his boyhood, or they have him mouthing philosophical gibberish that sounds peculiarly close to today's New Age beliefs (which may explain why some of these fake Gospels are being read again).

But even though the Bible says little about its own authority, many people are impressed by the Bible's seriousness. The introductory words "Thus says the Lord..." appear throughout it. Even when those exact words aren't used, the idea is there. The writers seem to have been convinced that they were indeed writing the dead-serious words that God had prompted them to write. You do not get the impression that the Bible authors were just trying to entertain or impress with their cleverness. It is as if the words they wrote were marked, "Take me seriously! Urgent!"

Still, the authority question can't be settled by the Bible itself. So what about human experience? Millions of people have, for centuries, believed the Bible was the word of God...and millions have not. You can't settle a matter like this by pointing out numbers. After all, most people in the past believed the world was flat, and they were wrong. But for what it's worth, many people—intellectuals, simple folk, rulers, authors, military leaders, philosophers, merchants, doctors—have believed that the Bible had divine authority. Some believed it along with other people whom they knew. Others went against the tide and believed in the Bible's authority in spite of the fact their belief made them unpopular. Some even became martyrs.

What Does *Inspiration* Mean?

Let's consider the matter of *inspiration*. The word *inspire* literally means "breathe in." The New Testament uses an interesting Greek word for this: *theopneustos*. It means "God-breathed." This doesn't mean God had a literal breath that created the Bible. It means the invisible, spiritual God is somehow "in" the Bible. The Bible came to exist because God was "in" the writing process. His power, his life, are represented by the figurative word "breath."

The apostle Paul wrote to Timothy, a young Christian pastor, "All Scripture is God-breathed and is useful for teaching, rebuking, correcting and training in righteousness, so that the man of God may be thoroughly equipped for every good work" (2 Timothy 3:16). ("Scripture" means the same as *Bible.*) Paul had a practical concept of the Bible. It was "God-breathed," but that didn't mean we should fall down and worship the book. It means the Bible's words are *useful.* They are God's way of training us to be the kind of people we're meant to be. Paul had no interest in "opening up sacred mysteries." He saw the Bible as God's manual for life. In another letter, Paul said that "everything that was written in the past was written to teach us, so that through endurance and the encouragement of the Scriptures we might have hope" (Romans 15:4).

Peter, author of two New Testament letters, made a high claim for the Bible's authority: "You must understand that no prophecy of Scripture came about by the prophet's own interpretation. For prophecy never had its origin in the will of man, but men spoke from God as they were carried along by the Holy Spirit" (2 Peter 1:20-21). Again, we read the idea of "God-breathed." Who wrote the words in the Bible? Human beings. Who gives the "life," the "breath," the "spirit" to the Bible? God.

There are some who have said that God simply dictated the Bible. In this view, the human authors were nothing more than secretaries—writing robots, you might say. But the Bible—either in a translation or in the original Greek and Hebrew—shows that the authors had very different styles of writing. Paul's letters are unmistakably Paul's. He had his own personality and writing style. If the human authors were merely robotic secretaries for God, then the whole Bible would sound the same. But God did not override or smother the individual writers' personalities. Rather, the authors were moved by God. We might say they felt an inward pressure or compulsion to write the words that God wished to communicate to the world.

This is what is meant by inspiration—a hard concept to explain, as you may have noticed. It can't be proven scientifically. But many people—some simple, some brilliant—have believed it. They believed that Jesus was, in some unexplainable way, both fully human and fully divine. They believed similarly about the Bible. It was produced by living, breathing human beings. It was produced by the power of a God who wished to reveal himself. The Bible's origin is both human and divine.

Now, you can believe that Shakespeare's *Hamlet* is an inspired work. You can believe that God gave Shakespeare his talent, his genius. You can believe that there is truth in *Hamlet*. But this isn't the same as God-breathed. Believing the Bible is God-breathed means believing that it—the whole Bible, not just the portions we enjoy, or portions that fit well with contemporary thought—is God's word to the entire human race.

What Does *Inerrancy* Mean?

Bible scholars have long quarreled over the matter of inspiration, and they also argue about something called *inerrancy*. To say something is *inerrant* is to say it's without error. It has no mistakes—none.

I personally believe the Bible is inerrant. By this I mean that, in terms of spiritual and eternal matters, it is always correct. But I will be honest: It contains difficult passages. For example, the four Gospels report different things about the women who find Jesus' grave empty. Mark's Gospel says, "As they entered the tomb, they saw a young man dressed in a white robe sitting on the right side, and they were alarmed" (Mark 16:5). Luke's Gospel reads, "While they were wondering about this, suddenly two men in clothes that gleamed like lightning stood beside them" (Luke 24:4). Which is right? One man inside the tomb, or two men near the tomb? The Gospels are apparently describing angels—but one angel, or two?

These kinds of discrepancies bother some people. They shouldn't. Think of four people you deeply trust, and ask all four to report something that they all witnessed. You will hear about the same event, but their views on that event may differ in the details. (You may gain more from having four witnesses rather than just having one.)

Also, we have to consider the copying process: We learn from Bible scholars that the ancient manuscripts agree on most things, but not all. In the process of thousands of copies being written, changes occurred. Those old pieces of papyrus agree on all the important things, yet they do disagree about minor things. Looking at how extremely similar all the copies are, you might conclude that God was overseeing the process. You might also conclude that, yes, human beings do make mistakes.

DIGGING ARCHAEOLOGY

Do altars have horns? The Old Testament claims that certain people held on to the "horns of the altar" (1 Kings 1:50; 2:28), and readers puzzled over just what these "horns" were. Archaeologists have uncovered altars that actually do have triangular projections on the corner—projections that are just like horns. (You might notice in the Old Testament that an animal horn is often a symbol of power.)

Do such "errors" mean the Bible is untrustworthy? Why would it? If your spouse leaves a mess in the kitchen and runs off to play tennis, do you conclude that he or she is completely selfish and unloving? No, not if you have a lot of other evidence to the contrary.

Besides these minor discrepancies, we need to keep in mind that those who wrote the Bible described natural phenomena in language that was available to them. They weren't fabricating details. Rather, they were describing things from their limited human perspective. For example, we ourselves use an inaccurate expression all the time: We say the sun rises and sets. We know full well it doesn't. Another example is Genesis 7:11, which describes the great flood in Noah's day and says, "the floodgates of the heavens were opened." Was the author saying the sky has gates? No, he was simply communicating how heavily it rained.

When we read statements that seem inaccurate, it helps to do research so we can understand the reason for the statement. For example, in Mark 4:31, Jesus compares the kingdom of God to the mustard seed and says this seed "is the smallest seed you plant in the ground." Strictly speaking, he was wrong. Many plants have seeds smaller than the mustard seed. But Bible scholars point out the words "smallest seed you plant in the ground." In other words, it was the smallest seed of the plants farmers purposely planted for food. Also, Jesus was speaking to people in ancient Israel. Of the seeds grown at that time by farmers in that part of the world, the mustard seed was the smallest.

There are some things in the Bible we cannot take *literally*. For example, when Jesus said, "I am the bread of life," no one took this to mean he could be cut up and spread with butter. When he told his disciples, "I am the vine; you are the branches," none of them expected to grow leaves. The New Testament says many times that the resurrected Jesus is now seated at the right hand of God. Literally? No. The Bible makes it clear that God is a spirit, not a body with a right hand. The authors meant that Jesus is with God—and not just with him, but in close fellowship with him as God's "right-hand man," to use our modern phrase. (When we call

George Washington "the Father of our country," everyone knows we don't mean it literally, right?)

Sometimes the words spoken by people in the Bible were misunderstood. Jesus told the inquisitive Nicodemus, "No one can see the kingdom of God unless he is born again" (John 3:3). Poor Nicodemus! He asked Jesus just how that was literally possible. We chuckle. Nicodemus was too literal-minded. Didn't he know Jesus was talking about a *spiritual* rebirth?

But, take note: Most parts of the Bible *were* meant to be taken literally. When the Old Testament says that the Assyrian king Sennacherib made war on Judah, it means it. In fact, the Old and New Testaments refer to many solid, historical facts. Archaeologists continually find new evidence that the Bible authors had their facts straight. There was a real Assyrian King Sennacherib, and he really did make war on Judah. Most of the Bible takes place in this literal, historical world. Saying the Bible is a "spiritual" book is true. But it is full of history, too—hard data and real events. The Old and New Testaments are about God acting in history.

Other things were meant to be taken literally. That includes the miracles. And that includes the great miracle of Jesus being raised from the dead. This miracle is mentioned again and again in the New Testament. There is not a hint that anyone understood it figuratively. The writers themselves did not think this was a legend. Jesus' followers really did believe that, somehow, the body that had

DIGGING ARCHAEOLOGY

The Old Testament mentions an Egyptian Pharaoh named Shishak (or Sheshonk), who attacked Jerusalem in the time of King Rehoboam (2 Chronicles 12:2). Archaeologists have found Shishak's record of this military campaign inscribed on a wall in a temple in Karnak in Egypt. The Bible claims that he did not capture Jerusalem, but imposed a heavy tribute on the people there. The record in Egypt says exactly the same thing.

died and was buried was alive again. It was somehow like his old body, but different, too. You may not believe this. But if you read the New Testament, you have to conclude that the early Christians really did believe it. Some paid the price of their lives for believing it. Would they have died for an illusion, for a figurative resurrection? No. They believed that a real historical event had occurred: Jesus did rise from the dead.

DIGGING ARCHAEOLOGY

The Bible records the Babylonian king Nebuchadnezzar's siege of Jerusalem in this way:

> Nebuchadnezzar himself came up to the city while his officers were besieging it. Jehoiachin king of Judah...his nobles and his officials all surrendered to him. In the eighth year of the reign of the king of Babylon, he took Jehoiachin prisoner.... Nebuchadnezzar removed all the treasures from the temple of the LORD and from the royal palace, and took away all the gold articles...Nebuchadnezzar took Jehoiachin captive to Babylon.... He made Mattaniah, Jehoiachin's uncle, king in his place and changed his name to Zedekiah (2 Kings 24:11-13,15,17).

Archaeologists found a Babylonian clay tablet confirming these exact details.

What About Infallibility?

Back to inerrancy: Believing the Bible is error-free means that *in all matters of faith, the Bible is true.* To be concise, we call this *infallibility.* The early Christians believed that Jesus' resurrection was a key point of faith. They believed he really had died, risen, and been taken into heaven. They believed that if they trusted him, they would spend eternity with him in their own new and resurrected bodies. These things can't be scientifically proven nor disproven. Rather, it comes down to faith. Accept the Bible as the inspired, authoritative word of God, or don't. To accept this doesn't mean you have to ignore the fact there are some portions that are difficult to understand. All you have to accept is that "the holy Scriptures...are able to make you wise for salvation through faith in Christ Jesus" (2 Timothy 3:15). In the Bible's view, salvation is Priority #1. And we need to remember this: People are not saved by the Bible. People are saved by God.

One very old statement of faith claims that the Bible "contains all things necessary for salvation." That's a nice summary. It doesn't say the Bible is a science textbook or an encyclopedia, but a "salvation handbook." The one thing it is supposed to do—reveal the saving truth of God—it does perfectly well.

One more item: The Christian view is that the Bible sets the boundaries of belief. Any belief that is truly *Christian* has to be based on the clear teachings in the Bible. Unlike Hinduism and that wide group of beliefs called New Age, the faith presented in the Bible isn't open to any idea that seems vaguely "spiritual." So if you base your beliefs on the Bible, you can be environmentally conscious, but you can't worship nature. You can't practice channeling, or dabble in the occult, or try to get in touch with your past incarnations, or worship Mother Earth, or call yourself a pagan or neo-pagan, or believe that you yourself are God. The Bible sets a wall around belief. This isn't a wall to keep you from anything good. It's a wall to keep out garbage.

What Is a *Canon*?

Canon is the word the scholars use to refer to the 66 books included in the Bible. It means "rule" or "standard," and the idea is that the 66 books of the Bible are the definitive holy writings for believers. The canon—the Bible as a whole—is God's word to man. Other writings besides the Bible may seem inspired, but only the Bible itself is holy, separate, and distinct from all other writings.

Though the whole Bible is *inspired,* that doesn't mean every part of it is *inspiring.* Millions of readers through the centuries have been touched by Jesus' wonderful Sermon on the Mount (Matthew 5–7).

THE BIBLE AND THE QUR'AN:
BOTH INSPIRED?

All the great world religions have their sacred writings. In our own day, none is perhaps as significant in world events as the Qur'an, the holy book of the Muslims. Any TV news broadcast or newspaper will convince you that the Qur'an is by no means a "dead" book. Millions of Muslims across the world take it very seriously. In fact, the devotion many Muslims feel for the Qur'an is intense compared to what many so-called Christians feel for the Bible.

In contrast to the Bible, the Qur'an (often spelled Koran, by the way) was a one-man production. The sole writer was the prophet Muhammad himself. According to Muslim belief, Muhammad was a sort of "channel" for the words of Allah (God). In the Muslim view, Allah simply used Muhammad as a secretary. Every word of the Qur'an was written by Muhammad, and so this book was written in the life span of one individual.

The Bible, compared to the Qur'an, seems like more of a hodge-podge—a miniature of history, law, poetry, prophecy, letters, parables. Its authors are numerous. It was written over a period of centuries. It was not only a group effort, but also a trans-historical effort.

There is something else that sets the Bible apart from the Qur'an: the tendency to ask questions of the Almighty. The Bible is authoritative, presenting God as the world's lawgiver and ruler. And parts of the Bible are direct commands. But the Bible also shows human beings in dialogue with God. The wonderful book of Job shows a saintly man agonizing and asking God why he allows a good person to suffer. The prophet Habakkuk raises similar questions. The book of Ecclesiastes has its author wrestling with a universal question: Is life ultimately meaningless, or does our devotion to God give it meaning? God, in the Bible, is the Almighty (like Allah in the Qur'an). He is also one who allows man to argue with him. In the Bible, it is okay to ask God, "Why?"

There is another contrast: the Bible's portrayal of saints who were also sinners. Their stories fascinate us. King David of Israel is a great man—he was a musician, poet, warrior, and devoted man of God. He was also an adulterer, overly indulgent father, and sometimes a downright rogue. Abraham, a man of faith, was sometimes a phenomenal liar. Moses freed the people of Israel from slavery in Egypt, aided by his devoted brother and sister—who later rebel against him.

Are these just amusing stories? Or is there some benefit of seeing God and man portrayed in stories? Instead of just laws and commands, the Bible also gives us pictures—pictures of human beings engaged in relationship with God. The Bible gives us statements such as, "Do not murder" and "God is love." But it also tells us stories that show *how* God is love and how bad things result from murder. No wonder some people have called the Bible "the Book of the Acts of God."

So perhaps there is something to be said for a multitude of authors. They all witness, in their different ways, to the acts of God.

Not many people will admit to being inspired by the laws for animal sacrifices in Leviticus 5–6. The book of Job is beautiful and touching, sensitive in its exploration of human questions about suffering and justice. The book of Esther is…well, an interesting (but violent and vindictive) story about a particular incident in Jewish history.

Some people have their own "canon within the canon." Entire books have been written on Matthew's Gospel, the Psalms, and Paul's letter to the Romans. Pastors have preached great series of sermons on the book of Isaiah and the book of Acts. But not much attention is given to the Song of Solomon or the tiny book of Obadiah. Some readers say it's because those books aren't very useful for their lives. But the Bible as a whole is a useful book, even though not all parts seem equally useful. The Bible needs to be taken as a whole, and not selectively. We shouldn't read and reread some parts and neglect others.

Since the very beginnings of Christianity, people have been tempted to "cut and paste" their own Bible, tossing out parts they don't find appealing. Thomas Jefferson, for example, was a highly moral man, but he couldn't swallow the miracle stories in the Gospels. So he put together his own New Testament, which edited out the miracles. (That left a crucified, buried, but not risen Jesus.) Early in Christian history a man named Marcion edited his own Bible. He threw out the entire Old Testament and some of the New. Why? He didn't like the "angry" God, the God as Judge depicted in some parts of the Bible. He liked the images of God as a loving Father

DIGGING ARCHAEOLOGY

John's Gospel mentions a healing at the Pool of Bethesda in Jerusalem. According to John, this pool had five porches. For centuries, no one found evidence of any such place. Then in 1888 diggers found the remains of a public bathhouse in Jerusalem that had five porches (colonnades).

(don't we all?) but felt that they didn't fit with the "darker" images of God. He thought Christianity would be an easier sell if it threw out the "bad God" and left only the "good God." But Christians as a whole said, "No. You can't just pick and choose the parts you like. You can't create a god of your own liking. You have to accept the God of the whole Bible."

And, as it happened, Marcion is one of the main reasons we have a canon of 66 books. Radical individualists such as Marcion prodded Christians to put their heads together and decide, once and for all, just what writings were holy Scripture.

When the New Testament mentions Scripture (as in 2 Timothy 3:16—"All Scripture is God-breathed"), it refers to the Old Testament, which the church honored as God's word for mankind. But while the young church was growing, the New Testament as we know it was not considered holy Scripture—not yet anyway, for it was still being written.

The New Testament itself indicates that early Christians were starting to regard the Gospels and Paul's epistles as special in some way. In 2 Peter 3:16 is a notable reference to Paul's writings—Peter said that Paul's epistles are sometimes "hard to understand." But Paul's wisdom is described as God-given, and Peter chides the "ignorant and unstable people" who distort Paul's words—as they distort *other* Scriptures. So by the time 2 Peter was written, there was already awareness among Christians that holy writings other than the Old Testament were available for inspiring the faithful.

The idea of a canon (or standard) began to develop. The Jews had established that some books—the Old Testament—were clearly inspired by God. In regard to the New Testament, Christians felt the same need to distinguish between truly inspired writings and those that were questionable. What were the guidelines these Christians had in mind as they began to formulate the New Testament canon?

One was *apostolic origin*. After the apostles died, it was natural that the later generations would value their witness in writing. Paul was an apostle—though not one of the original Twelve, his zeal and missionary activity made him the very model of an apostle. So the

DIGGING ARCHAEOLOGY

The book of Acts records a strange scene: The Christian missionaries Paul and Barnabas preach and heal in the town of Lystra, and the local people believe the missionaries are the gods Zeus and Hermes. The local priest of Zeus tries to sacrifice some bulls to the visiting "gods" (Acts 14).

Archaeologists find that, indeed, Lystra had a Zeus-and-Hermes fixation. Near the town they found a statue of the god Hermes and a stone altar dedicated to both Zeus and Hermes.

letters from Paul were viewed as apostolic and thus inspired, as 2 Peter indicates. The Gospels—and there were many that did not make it into the New Testament—had to be attached to some apostle. Thus we have Matthew and John. But what about Luke and Mark, who were not apostles? Mark's Gospel was associated with Peter, and Luke's was associated with Paul. So an apostle did not have to *be* the author so long as an apostolic connection was established.

The bulk of the writings in our New Testament were authored by apostles—Paul (his many letters), Matthew (his Gospel), Peter (two letters), and John (his Gospel, three letters, and most likely Revelation). Surprisingly, two of the four Gospels were not by apostles, but the authors had "connections." Mark, mentioned several times in the New Testament, was supposed to have been a fellow worker with the apostle Peter. So Mark's Gospel is not by an apostle but is based on the testimony of one of the key apostles, Peter. Likewise, Luke was not an apostle but was a close associate of the apostle Paul. Luke wrote not only his Gospel, but also Acts, and some parts of Acts (the "we" passages) are written by Luke as eyewitness accounts.

The upshot: The New Testament was written by Jesus' apostles or by people who knew the apostles well. It was written by people who could say, "I know about this because I was there."

Another guideline was *the writings' use in the churches.* An operating principle seemed to be, "If a lot of churches use this writing and it continues to enlighten them, it must be inspired." In others words, if something is inspired by God, it will, no doubt, inspire many people. So a writing that God had not inspired would inevitably, over time, fall out of use.

But these concerns did not settle the issue of what books would finally be established as the canon. For one thing, there were many books attributed to apostles, and some of these writings were blatantly heretical—that is, not in keeping with the true gospel. And churches in some locales used writings that other churches did not care to use.

Yet there was still some consistency among the churches. By the end of the second century, the four Gospels, Acts, and Paul's epistles were honored almost everywhere. There was no "official" list, but, rather, an unofficial "grassroots" consensus that these writings had spiritual authority. But while these were generally seen as inspired, there was much dispute over some—Hebrews, James, 2 Peter, 2 and 3 John, Jude, and Revelation.

Heresy has a way of making orthodox believers clarify their position. The necessity of an official canon became clear as notable heretics established their own canons. As far as we know, the first attempt at a canon was that of the heretic Marcion, whose canon included only ten epistles of Paul and a heavily edited Gospel of Luke. Later heretical

DIGGING ARCHAEOLOGY

In Acts 17:6, Luke uses the odd word *politarchs* to refer to the authorities in the Greek city of Thessalonica. (The word is translated "city officials" in most English Bibles.) Historians used to believe this was just a word Luke had made up. They had never run across this word anywhere else but in Acts. But archaeologists eventually found an ancient archway in Thessalonica with the inscription "In the days of the politarchs…." Luke had been perfectly correct in using this word.

groups cherished their own special "secret books" (usually circulated with an apostle's name attached so as to lend authority). As a result, the faithful could see that an orthodox canon was needed. (Many of these books are now called Apocryphal gospels and epistles. Their picture of Jesus is usually quite different from the Jesus we meet in the four Gospels of the New Testament.)

In A.D. 367 the influential bishop of Alexandria, Athanasius, penned a widely circulated Easter letter. In it he listed the 27 books that we now have in the New Testament. The list was intended to be exclusive. Athanasius, hoping to guard his flock from heresy, stated that no other books could be regarded as Christian Scripture, though he allowed that some others might be useful for private devotions.

Athanasius' letter did not settle the matter completely. There was still dispute over certain books—Hebrews, James, 2 Peter, and 2 and 3 John, and Jude. But eventually the Christian world did accept all 27 books, excluding all others. Scattered groups of heretics continued to cherish their pet writings, but these heretical writings did not gain universal acceptance. Athanasius' list has indeed become the canon—the standard—and the churches throughout the world have not seriously deviated from his wisdom.

The Bible we have is the result of "community consensus" as opposed to "radical individualism." Christians have generally assumed that the consensus came because of the Holy Spirit's guidance.

So beware of too much individualism. God loves each individual, but Christianity has never been a "private" religion—"just me, the Bible, and God." An individual can have brilliant insights as well as completely kooky ideas. If you're striving for individuality and nonconformity, be aware that you could be missing something. The Bible has been around for centuries. Many wise people have read it, studied it, interpreted it. And their insights have been passed on to other Christians. And other writers have been crackpots. Their ideas do, in the course of time, get tossed aside.

BROWS HIGH AND LOW

Is the Bible for airheads? Eggheads? Or is it for everyone?

In the New Testament, the apostle Paul (an educated man, a thinker) said to some of the Christians, "Brothers, think of what you were when you were called. Not many of you were wise by human standards; not many were influential; not many were of noble birth" (1 Corinthians 1:26).

Paul (who was not being unkind, just honest) was aware that the first Christians were not intellectuals—not many of them, anyway. In fact, in the first few years of the new faith, very few intellectuals were attracted to it. (One early Christian, Apollos, is called "a learned man" in Acts 18:24.) Most intellectuals then saw Christianity as just another silly superstition—and the Roman Empire was full of them at that time. This rejection by the "brain elite" didn't bother the early Christians at all. They believed the faith was real—and if the highbrows rejected it, well, what did it matter?

But the intellectuals' attitude changed. Some were won over to the new faith. They were attracted not only to its morals and its belief in an afterlife, but to its teachings. Some of them tossed aside the pagan philosophies they had held to and embraced the Bible. This was, they thought, the real Ultimate Truth they had been pursuing so long. This new belief system seemed to "hang together" in a way their old philosophies didn't. By the year A.D. 300 (around the time Emperor Constantine made Christianity a legal religion), many of the great intellects in the Roman Empire were Christians.

Has anything changed in 1600 years? Are there uneducated, semi-literate people today who claim to believe in the Bible? Of course—and why not, since the Bible never makes any claim to being just a book for intellectuals? But are there intellectuals in our own day who believe the Bible? Or do they say the old Book is past its prime?

It isn't, and yes, there are plenty of intelligent, well-educated people who believe the Bible. But rather than listing some contemporary people who fit this category, consider what other beliefs have become acceptable among well-educated people:

channeling

reincarnation

astral projection

astrology

crystals

earth worship

goddess worship

self-worship

UFO abductions

4

Meaning What?

INTERPRETING
THE BIBLE

Reading the Bible is a lot like reading someone else's mail. In the case of the many letters in the New Testament, this is literally true. As sometimes happens when we read someone else's mail, we may not understand everything we read. Some obvious questions to ask are: Who sent this? Who received it? What was the purpose of the letter? What incidents caused the letter to be sent? How is the recipient expected to respond?

This last question is the key one. You see, the books of the Old and New Testaments weren't sent to us...and yet they were. Christians know that Paul sent the original letter to the Romans to the Christians at Rome in the first century A.D. Yet Christians believe that this letter, like all parts of the Bible, is addressed to us also. If it is not, then we study the Bible only out of curiosity (which is a valid reason, but not one that many people choose). If the book of Exodus was written for the ancient Hebrews—and *only* for them—then why study it today? If we read the Bible solely out of curiosity, wouldn't we get as much (or more) pleasure from reading a Tom Clancy novel or a Dave Barry humor column?

So Bible readers have a two-pronged task: interpret the Bible (What does it mean?) and apply the Bible (What does it mean *to me and how I live my life?*). This is what makes the Bible different from other ancient writings such as Homer's *Odyssey* or Sophocles' *Oedipus Rex*. We can read and try to interpret *The Odyssey*. But we don't follow up by asking, How will this now affect my life? Homer and Sophocles never included the words "Thus says the Lord" or "Thus say the gods" in their writings. (Since we don't believe in the Greek gods Zeus and Hermes, what Homer's *Iliad* says about them isn't too important for us today.) But the Bible, in many, many places, uses the phrase "Thus says the Lord...." It is clear that the Bible authors believed they were saying something with a divine origin. And if it was divine, it had to affect human life. You could not read it and then reply, "So what?"

An Age of Confusion

You don't have to be brilliant or well-educated to read and understand the Bible. Jesus himself made this clear: "I praise you, Father, Lord of heaven and earth, because you have hidden these things from the wise and learned, and revealed them to little children" (Matthew 11:25). Jesus didn't mean that the truth was off-limits to the wise. He meant that it was possible for anyone with an open mind—even a child—to understand the truth.

In the early days of Christianity, most people could read. They had access to the books we now call the Old Testament, and also to the writings that eventually were collected as the New Testament. But after about A.D. 500, literacy declined. This was the period historians called the Dark Ages—not literally dark, but a bad period for learning and literacy. During this period the Bible continued to be read and copied. But the average Christian (who probably could not read anyway) had no access to the Bible. The people who had Bibles were priests and the monks who lived secluded lives in monasteries. Here they did something important: They copied Bibles so that future generations would have them.

But they did something else: They wrote commentaries on the Bible. They weren't writing these commentaries for the average reader (and remember, the average person couldn't read anyway), but for themselves. There was a sort of "Bible elite," the sheltered monks who spent their days studying and copying the Bible and writing books about it.

Some of their commentaries dazzle us. They weren't satisfied with just reading the Bible and discovering what it meant and how to apply it to life. They wanted to go "beyond the surface"—to discover the *hidden* meanings of the Bible.

DOES GOD HAVE FINGERS?

God is an invisible spirit, but the Bible sometimes speaks figuratively of God's bodily parts: "When the LORD finished speaking to Moses on Mount Sinai, he gave him the two tablets of the Testimony, the tablets of stone inscribed by the finger of God" (Exodus 31:18). So the mysterious "fiery finger" depicted in the movie *The Ten Commandments* is perhaps not as far-fetched as we might think.

An example: the word *water*. When you run across this word in the Bible, you probably assume it means just what it says: water—that wet, clear stuff we drink and bathe in. But the Bible elite of the Dark Ages said, "No, that's only the literal meaning. It must mean more than that." They interpreted the word *allegorically* and said that it meant baptism. They interpreted it *morally* and said it meant sorrow (or wisdom, or heresy, or prosperity). They interpreted it *spiritually* and said it meant eternal happiness. These three "senses," they said, were the "real" meaning of the word, much more interesting than reading it *literally* (the fourth "sense"). And you thought water was just water!

Another example: In Genesis 1:3 God says, "Let there be light." Literally, this means God created light. But to these commentators, allegorically, it means "let Christ be love." Morally, it means "let us be illuminated by Christ." Spiritually, it means "let us be led to heaven by Christ." (And you thought it just meant that God had created light.) For the name *Jerusalem,* they had these four interpretations: literally, the old city named Jerusalem; allegorically, the church; morally, the human soul; spiritually, heaven.

Note: Some pagan intellectuals applied the same methods of interpretation to other ancient writings such as *The Iliad* and *The Odyssey*. These types of "experts" feel the need to come up with something new and clever, and not just pass on old traditions. (You can see this today in colleges, where professors find all kinds of new and radical meanings in authors such as Shakespeare and Jane Austen.)

The early Bible experts were especially fervent to apply their fourfold interpretative method to the Old Testament. With so many stories of tribal wars, rebellions, and other unpleasant subjects, the interpreters couldn't take these violent tales at face value. There has to be, they said, a deeper meaning, an allegorical-moral-spiritual meaning. The literal meaning of Joshua's armies invading Canaan was not important. Nor were the blatantly sensuous poems in the Song of Solomon. (This book was a particular favorite of interpreters, who firmly believed that these poems about male-female attraction just *had* to have a spiritual meaning. What is interesting is that these Bible experts in the Middle Ages were men who had taken a vow of celibacy. No wonder they couldn't take the Song of Solomon at face value!)

There was one advantage of interpreting the Bible in these "fantastic" ways: None of the Bible went to waste. By assuming that every verse in the Bible had a "deeper" meaning, the Bible elite could find meanings in the most unlikely places—the laws of sacrifice in Leviticus, the measurements of the temple in Ezekiel, the censuses of Israel in Numbers. Taken literally, these passages don't seem to have much meaning for us today. But the Bible elite of the Middle Ages could find *many* meanings—even if those meanings really had nothing to do with the passage! Yet by finding meaning in every verse, they were able to "use" the whole Bible—there were no "leftovers," no verses without some importance.

Does all this sound like a sort of intellectual word game? It was. But to give these men credit, some of them were probably trying to find real spiritual meaning in the Bible. Believing that the whole Bible had real meaning for people in every time and place, these interpreters sought to find that meaning. They assumed (probably correctly) that most readers want to know about God and themselves, but are not terribly interested in the Canaanites or the prophet Ezekiel.

But most of these scholars were caught up in their own cleverness, eager to put a new spin on some Bible verse that had been interpreted cleverly before. It was a case of "Can you top this?" Common folk might read a Bible passage and accept it "as is." But many of these intellectuals believed that such literal reading was a "surface" reading that overlooked the "deeper" meaning—that is, a meaning that the average person would not see. One noted Bible commentator of this period said, "The sense of God's Word is infinitely varied, and like a peacock's feather, it glows with many colors." (A modern comparison: Literary critics today talk about "feminist themes in Shakespeare" or "social beliefs in the novels of Charles Dickens." They are trying to make the old writings relevant to a new age. But they are missing the real point—and real beauty—of Shakespeare and Dickens.)

In the meantime, while these clever Bible scholars were finding new colors in the peacock's feather, the people in the churches were not benefitting. If they even heard the Bible being read in church, it was read in Latin, a language only the scholars understood. What is odd is that during the Middle Ages, everyone in Europe was a baptized Christian. Yet the average person lived and died without much exposure to the words and teachings of the Bible. The Bible elites pored over the Bible and found many meanings in it. But the average Christian really had no knowledge of *any* meaning of the Bible. The people in the pews depended on the priests and bishops and monks to do their thinking for them. And unfortunately, the priests rarely preached sermons on the Bible.

Change came with the Protestant Reformation in the 1500s. The Protestant leaders emphasized translating the Bible into people's own languages. They insisted that pastors preach sermons that explained the Bible to the people. And that amazing new invention, the printing press, helped make the Bible more available to everyone. With more books available, more people learned to read—often for the sole purpose of being able to read the Bible. For the first time in centuries, laymen—farmers, merchants, housewives, laborers—could read the Bible themselves. Because they lived in the real world and not the ivory-tower world of professional scholars, they took a common-sense approach to the Bible: What does this literally mean? they asked. That question has, thank heavens, dominated Bible study ever since.

The Literal Meaning

Even during those centuries when interpreters were finding all kinds of obscure meanings in the Bible, some voices of sense prevailed. Emphasize the literal meaning, they said. Try to discern what the author was trying to communicate.

But can we take the whole Bible *literally?* Consider these verses, which are God speaking to the patriarch Abraham:

> He [God] took him [Abraham] outside and said, "Look up at the heavens and count the stars—if indeed you can count them." Then he said to him, "So shall your offspring be" (Genesis 15:5).

> I will surely bless you and make your descendants as numerous as the stars in the sky and as the sand on the seashore (Genesis 22:17).

Now, if God is truly the all-knowing One, he would know the number of the stars in the sky and the grains of sand on the seashore. Abraham didn't, and neither do we. Based on what scientists tell us, the sands on the seashore are a huge number—and definitely a larger number than Abraham's descendants, the Hebrews/Israelites/Jews.

So was God amiss in his promise to Abraham? Of course not. God didn't mean for the promise to be taken literally. Abraham's descendants haven't grown in number to equal the number of stars or grains of sand. The message of the promise was this: "I will give you many, many descendants—so many that you would think of them as innumerable." In other words, this is poetic exaggeration for the sake of making a point. And it is more memorable than if God had simply said, "I will give you lots and lots of descendants." (We say, "It's raining cats and dogs," and no one takes it literally. That sounds more interesting than simply saying, "It's raining very hard.")

Other passages in the Bible are obviously not meant to be taken literally. Jesus made several statements about himself that were not meant literally: "I am the bread of life" (John 6:48), "I am the light of the world" (John 8:12), "I am the gate for the sheep" (John 10:7), "I am the true vine, and my Father is the gardener" (John 15:1). Did he mean he was literally bread, or light, or a gate, or a vine? Of course not. He was speaking figuratively, with a spiritual meaning. Usually it is very obvious when you are dealing with such a passage. (When you read about the Confederate general "Stonewall" Jackson, you probably do not assume he was actually made of stone. Why? Because we recognize that is a figurative name. He was called "Stonewall" because of his grit and determination.)

The Bible also speaks of God's "body," yet makes it clear that God is a spiritual being without a body. Many times, especially in the Old Testament, we read about the hand, eyes, ears, or even the nostrils of the Lord. The Bible writers knew that God does not have literal body parts. They were expressing as best they could some important ideas: God knows things (eyes and ears), and he has power to act (hand and arm). When describing an indescribable spiritual being, we have to use words people understand—even if those words are poetic or symbolic and not literal.

Let's take another example: hell. Jesus said, "The Son of Man will send out his angels, and they will weed out of his kingdom everything that causes sin and all who do evil. They will throw them into the fiery furnace, where there will be weeping and gnashing of teeth" (Matthew 13:41-42). Let's interpret: Jesus spoke of himself as "the Son of Man," so there's no confusion about this. What about the "fiery furnace" and the "weeping and gnashing of teeth"? He is apparently talking about the fate of people who are not part of his kingdom. Will they be in a literal fire, grinding their literal teeth?

Probably not. If you say, "Joe's wife left him, and she broke his heart," does this mean his heart literally cracked open? No. You're saying, figuratively, that his wife caused him a great deal of internal pain. The same with the "fiery furnace." Jesus was communicating that sinners would be disposed of like something tossed away in a trash-burner. "Weeping and gnashing of teeth" are what people in agony would do, of course. If hell isn't literally a place of fire, it is something equally serious: a place where human beings end up being separated from God. Jesus said hell is a real place, even if his words about a fiery furnace are only figurative. It is no less true for being figurative.

So not every verse in the Bible can be taken literally.

Searching for the Bible's literal meanings means going for the obvious and finding out what the original writers intended to communicate to their readers. That's the first step. Finding out how that applies to us today is the second step. You must take the first before you take the second.

Is There Really a Hidden Meaning?

The last few paragraphs have been driving home a key point: It's important to read the Bible "as is" and find the most obvious meaning that the writers intended.

But we have to be honest: The Bible writers themselves found "hidden" or "spiritual" meanings within the Bible. You will notice this if you spend any time with the New Testament. The writers were quite capable of reading the Old Testament "as is." But they also found deeper meanings in it—meanings that the original Old Testament authors probably were unaware of. Quite often, the New Testament writers found that parts of the Old Testament applied to the life of Jesus. If your Bible has footnotes, you will notice this in the New Testament. On practically every page you'll see notes referring you to passages in the Old Testament. Why? Either the author is quoting the Old Testament directly, or at least making a passing reference to it.

Here is an example: Matthew's Gospel (2:18) quotes this passage from the Old Testament's book of Jeremiah: "A voice is heard in Ramah, weeping, and great mourning, Rachel weeping for her children and refusing to be comforted, because they are no more." The footnote tells you this is found in Jeremiah 31:15. If you look up that passage in Jeremiah, you'll find it in the middle of a passage about the Jews being abused by the Babylonians. Rachel was the wife of Jacob (also named *Israel,* who was the father of the 12 tribes of Israel). In the Jeremiah passage, "weeping for her children" meant Rachel was mourning for her descendants, who had been cruelly treated by the Babylonians. (See pages 22-26 for more information on footnotes in the Bible.)

But Matthew uses Jeremiah's words in this way: He's referring to evil King Herod, who slaughtered all the male infants of Bethlehem in an effort to kill the newborn Jesus. Matthew probably knew the literal meaning of Jeremiah 31:15. But when he told the story of Herod and the children, it struck him that the words of Jeremiah applied to the incident involving Herod. Jeremiah's words had been "fulfilled" by an incident in the life of Jesus. There's another way of looking at this: The slaughter of the infants by Herod *reminded* Matthew (painfully, we assume) of the verse in Jeremiah. It was as if Matthew remembered the verse and said, "Ah, that horrible incident concerning Herod certainly gives a new meaning to those words of Jeremiah."

Another example: In Luke's Gospel (22:37) Jesus quotes Isaiah 53:12: "He was numbered with the transgressors." Jesus goes on to say, "What is written about me is reaching its fulfillment." In short, Jesus himself read new meaning into the words of the Old Testament. Isaiah's words are part of what is called the "Suffering Servant Song," a poem about someone who suffers on other people's behalf. Was Isaiah making a prophecy, or just speaking about how an innocent person often suffers for others? We don't know. But apparently Jesus believed that Isaiah's words applied to him. This meant the words were now "fulfilled" by him.

One more example: The apostle Paul's sermon in Acts 13:35 quotes Psalm 16:10: "You will not let your Holy One see decay." If you look up Psalm 16, it isn't really a prophecy. It is the song of a moral person saying to God, "You will not let me die right now." It did not mean—so far as we can tell—that God would actually raise the man from the dead. But that is exactly what Paul means in Acts 13:35. He takes the verse from Psalm 16 and claims it has a deeper meaning—that it is "fulfilled" because Jesus, who is God's "Holy One," did not see decay but was raised from the dead.

This type of usage occurs repeatedly in the New Testament. The writers of the New Testament, who were familiar with the Old Testament, could not help noticing all these "coincidences." They believed that many passages from the Old Testament could now be read in a new light, since the life and work of Jesus had given them a new meaning.

So, when you read the Bible, first, try to find the most obvious literal meaning in any passage. But be prepared: Its own authors often found meanings beyond the obvious literal one. More about that later.

The "Fish Bone" Rule

When you read the Bible, you will find that most of it—let's say 75 percent—is pretty self-explanatory. You may stumble a bit over archaic-sounding names (such as Sennacherib or Nebuchadnezzar or Zedekiah), but these don't really affect your understanding of the text. But then there are passages that are hard to figure out.

Let's say you are reading the book of Exodus. Beginning at chapter 1, you read of the Israelites' slavery in Egypt. The Lord calls Moses, a shepherd, to lead the Israelites out of Egypt. Moses accepts the assignment and is on his way to Egypt. So far, so good—a pretty straightforward story.

But then you reach this odd passage: "At a lodging place on the way, the LORD met Moses and was about to kill him" (Exodus 4:24). Say what? Moses has just accepted God's assignment, and now God tries to kill him. Why? You read on. "But Zipporah [Moses' wife] took a flint knife, cut off her son's foreskin and touched Moses' feet with it. 'Surely you are a bridegroom of blood to me,' she said. So the LORD let him alone. (At that time she said 'bridegroom of blood,' referring to circumcision)" (Exodus 4:25-26).

You can look up this passage in a Bible commentary if you have one. But even the Bible scholars have trouble explaining these verses. We are faced with a rather obvious fact: When it comes to stories that were written thousands of years ago, *we cannot hope to understand every detail.* It's just not possible. Human nature is the same, and God is the same. But social customs and historical circumstances change. Many centuries separate us from Moses and his wife Zipporah. Most of Moses' story is perfectly clear, but Exodus 4:24-26 isn't—not even to the Bible scholars. The original writers must have understood it, but we don't.

So here's an option: Take a passage like this and set it aside. Treat it as you would a bone you find in a piece of fish. Lay it to the side of your plate and keep eating. Finding the bone in the fish shouldn't stop you from enjoying the rest of your dinner.

It is human nature to want to understand what we read. If you read a Stephen King or John Grisham novel, you can probably grasp just about everything in it. Of course you can—Stephen King knows how to write for people who think and speak the same as he does. You can't expect such complete clarity from something more than 2000 years old. (Does Stephen King expect his words to be selling well in 2000 years?)

So reading the Bible means putting aside the urge to understand every word. The old song says "accentuate the positive." In reading the Bible, you should "accentuate the understandable," or the parts you can grasp. A basic rule in Bible reading is to judge the unclear passages by the clear. You could, if you were new to the Bible, read Exodus 4:24-26 and conclude, "God is cruel. He calls Moses to serve him, then tries to kill him. God is unpredictable and mean!" You could conclude that, but it disagrees with the rest of the Bible, which shows God as faithful and loving. The Bible as a whole agrees with James 1:17, which speaks of God as "the Father of the heavenly lights, who does not change like shifting shadows." So, *judge the*

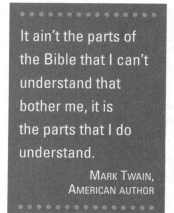

It ain't the parts of the Bible that I can't understand that bother me, it is the parts that I do understand.

MARK TWAIN,
AMERICAN AUTHOR

individual piece of the Bible by the whole Bible. This won't help you understand Exodus 4:24-26, but it will help you to "push it to the side of the plate." (Incidentally, I covered some of the most common "fish bones" in my book *What the Good Book Didn't Say: Popular Myths and Misconceptions About the Bible.*)

A word of warning: Don't apply the "fish bone" rule to passages that you happen not to like. If you happen to be committing adultery, or considering it, you probably won't like Exodus 20:14, "You shall not commit adultery." But *not liking* and *not understanding* are two different things. This commandment is perfectly clear. So are Jesus' words about the fiery furnace. They make it clear that hell is a real possibility for human beings. You may not like that idea, but Jesus' statement is clear and understandable. You can't treat it like a fish bone.

That brings us to an important point: The gap between us and the Bible's original audience is not as big as we might think. The fact is, the prophets in the Old Testament and Jesus and his apostles in the New were not always accepted or understood. Some people heard them gladly and responded with joy. But the majority did not. The faith of the Bible has always been a minority faith—not because people can't fathom it, but more often because they can fathom it and simply don't want to accept it. The Bible writers taught a high level of morality, and some people of their time responded to this by saying, "Yes, that's for me!" Others responded with "Killjoys! Fanatics! Puritans!" These same two responses are still around today. Some things never change.

A "Bowl of Fish Bones," the Book of Psalms

I admit that Psalms is my favorite book of the Old Testament. Many people across the centuries have agreed with me. Besides being the longest (150 psalms altogether), it is also the richest emotionally.

The 150 poems run the gamut of spiritual feeling—dejection, joy, doubt, ecstasy, anger, sorrow, gratitude. In all these poems the key character is the same: the God of Israel. Many of the psalms begin with the authors wallowing in negative feelings. But they always came back to the positive reality that God is in control of everything. Behind all the psalms—even the ones that express doubt or anger—is a strong belief in a God who is both just and merciful.

The Israelites and their descendants, the Jews, loved and still love the book of Psalms. More than any other book of the Old Testament it brings together the people's beliefs and feelings about their God. It was so well-loved by the Jews that the New Testament authors (most of whom were Jews) quoted it frequently. Jesus himself quoted from it many, many times. The early Christians accepted the book of Psalms as their own. They had no doubts that the psalms were holy and sacred, and they took them a step further than the Jews had: They saw many of the psalms as predictions of events in the life of Jesus. So they made Psalms a Christian book, and it was and still is a favorite book for Christians.

In the process of adopting the book as their own, the Christians often read into the text meanings that the original authors may not have intended. One example is the ending of the popular "shepherd psalm," Psalm 23: "I will dwell in the house of the LORD forever." As far as we can tell, the ending of the psalm, in the original Hebrew text meant, "I will live in the Lord's temple the rest of my life." The psalm did not seem to be talking about the afterlife, or heaven. (You'll find that that is actually a rare idea in the Old Testament.) But when the early Christians read the psalms, they couldn't help but find an "enriched" meaning in them. After all, the first Christians believed strongly in eternal life with God in heaven. So, when they read Psalm 23, they believed it had a new "fulfilled" meaning: "dwell in the house of the LORD forever" meant "live with God in heaven forever." You can argue whether it is right to "read in" a new meaning to part of the Old Testament. But Christians have done it for centuries, and it probably has done very little, if any, harm.

Unfortunately, the psalms are full of "fish bones" that cause some readers to choke. Since you probably will—and definitely should—read the book of Psalms, let's look at some of the things that cause readers problems.

Vindictiveness. The New Testament emphasizes loving our enemies and forgiving people who are cruel to us. Mercy is a Christian trait. But many of the psalms have a very different spirit. Some are even called "songs of vengeance." For example, Psalm 137 says, "O Daughter of Babylon, doomed to destruction, happy is he who repays you for what you have done to us—he who seizes your infants and dashes them against the rocks." Another example appears in Psalm 35: "Brandish spear and javelin against those who pursue me.... May those who seek my life be disgraced and put to shame; may those who plot my ruin be turned back in dismay" (verses 3-4). These are only two of many, many psalms that express the authors' rage. Instead of saying, "Lord, bless our enemies," these vengeful psalms say, "Crush them, Lord!"

From psalms such as these we sense that the authors were vengeful. Even worse, we picture God as vengeful also. Some of the psalm writers spoke as if God's purpose in the universe was to let loose his wrath on the writers' enemies.

A sensitive reader asks, What do we have to gain from reading these mean-spirited, un-Christian poems? One answer is to set them aside—like fish bones. You could do that, then go on to concentrate on psalms that are more inspiring.

But you can learn something from the vengeance psalms. First, you learn that expressing anger was socially acceptable in ancient times. In our civilization we try to keep our strong feelings to ourselves. (That may be changing, if you've watched politics in recent years.) In the ancient world, people were very blunt about their anger toward an enemy. And most often, the enemies in the psalms are not individual people, but whole nations—Egyptians, Babylonians, etc. From the vengeance psalms you can learn something about these nations: They were amazingly cruel (which archaeologists have confirmed). They were not only cruel as enemies, but even their worship services were primitive and cruel (some of them sacrificed children, for example). So it was natural, when Israel was threatened by these cruel nations, to say, "Smash them!" We may say this sounds cruel. Looked at another way, it meant that the Israelites had a deep sense of justice. They took right and wrong seriously, and that in itself is a very good thing.

We don't like the image of God as Judge. In our day we think that calling someone judgmental is one of the nastiest things we can say about a person. But the ancient Hebrews didn't see it that way. God the Divine Judge was the one who would bring justice—punishing the wicked, righting all wrongs, and releasing the good and rewarding them. As a small nation surrounded by larger (and crueler) nations, Israel had good reason to want this kind of justice. To an oppressed people stripped of many of their possessions, the news that the Judge was coming was wonderful news.

Self-righteousness. This is heartily condemned in the New Testament, notably by Jesus. It has no place in the Christian life. But it seems to show up in some of the psalms. Three examples: "I have kept the ways of the LORD; I have not done evil by turning from my God" (18:21). "Look upon my suffering and deliver me, for I have not forgotten your law" (119:153). "Judge me, O LORD, according to my righteousness, according to my integrity, O Most High" (7:8). Isn't this self-righteous boasting? Could a Christian pray these words? Didn't Jesus warn against such an attitude?

Yes, he did. We can think of these seemingly self-righteous passages as "fish bones." This is easy to do because so many other psalms are quite the opposite, with heartfelt confessions of sin. Psalm 51 is one of the greatest confessions in all the world's writings. It, and several others (notably 32 and 38), remind us that the true follower of God should be conscious of his own failings.

But, for the record, we can sympathize with the apparent self-righteousness in some of the psalms. Remember, the psalms weren't really used for a person's solitary reading. Rather, they were hymns used in group worship, usually at the temple in Jerusalem. When the psalms speak of "my righteousness" and "my integrity," the people were thinking in terms of "our righteousness." There was a strong "us" feeling in Israel, particularly because the people were God's chosen nation. Think of the self-righteousness this way: The nation of Israel, with all its faults, still compared well to the immoral and cruel nations around them.

Though psalms include some difficult content, that should not affect our enjoyment of them. They are full of assurances from God and reminders of His protective care for His people.

TWO THOUSAND YEARS AGO,
BUT FEELS LIKE NOW...

In your mind's eye, picture a society undergoing significant changes. This society was founded by people dedicated to freedom and equality. These people emphasized simple living and sneered at pomp and aristocracy. They wanted a society based on individual achievement, not inherited wealth. As this society grew and expanded, new lands were added. But all of them were included in this vision of freedom and equality.

Things changed. As time passed, the government began to promise the citizens more and more things. Most people still preferred to manage their own lives and create the good life by their own efforts. But an ever-expanding government became more eager to hand out "benefits." And the more that benefits were handed out, the greater the number of people who were willing to accept them. This society eventually became a magnet for the lazy and idle. This was especially true in the cities, which became miniature welfare states.

Art and literature changed. In the old days the authors and artists had been pretty restrained, hoping to inspire and entertain people in ways that would make no one blush. But decay set in. Many authors and artists chose to shock and titillate rather than to enlighten. Many sensitive people lamented the changes, but some government officials and wealthy people applauded the degraded art, and even bestowed government support on it.

The government could afford to be generous. As the society had grown, it had more people to tax. It could tax more and spend more. The beneficiaries of the spending applauded—and begged for more. After all, wasn't the government like a doting parent with limitless resources?

Entertainment had also become an obsession. The society in its young days had leisure time, but it emphasized hard work, too. The society in decay emphasized play. Professional sports were on everyone's mind, and egotistical pro athletes became overpaid heroes. This went along with a general focus on the body. People became fanatical about what they ate. Some people gorged themselves when they could, while others went to great lengths to have a youthful figure.

In the area of morals, relativism became the rule. The old rules governing business ethics and sexual morals became less popular. Some pro-tradition voices were heard, but as time passed the rule was...no rule. A "do your own thing" attitude pervaded moral choices. The ideas of restraint and self-denial seemed old-fashioned. The old norm of a close-knit family that passed on the old morals fell by the wayside.

And religion? There were many choices scattered across a wide spectrum of beliefs and moralities. The society had no one religion that bound it together, and no longer even a system of core beliefs that everyone accepted. Any new teacher of religion or philosophy could get a hearing in the marketplace of ideas. Some would not be accepted, but most could find a loyal following. So across the society, and especially in the urban centers, every form of religion prospered—goddess worship, nature worship, astrology, channeling, reincarnation, pantheism, and, perhaps most popular of all, a glorified self-centeredness that cast a halo around every individual's desires. If you read polls, you would get the impression the people were very religious. But even probing deeper, you would find that their beliefs were all over the map.

One rule held true in the sphere of religion: ABTOR—Anything But The Old Religion. People were confused about religion, but they weren't confused about their opinion that the old religious orthodoxy of the society's founders was boring, old-fashioned, not worth considering. A few tradition-minded people said, "No, the old beliefs are still valid." But they were now a tiny minority. Around them swirled a sea of strange and conflicting beliefs and moral attitudes.

What society is—or was—this? It could be our own today, or the Roman Empire of the New Testament period. You see, after 2000 years, we still live in the New Testament world. The world of the Old Testament is like our own, yet in some ways so radically different. But lay aside the differences in technology, and we're basically the same people as those who lived in the New Testament era.

One key difference between these two worlds is that in their day, the "old religion" that was scorned was the old belief system of the Roman Republic. In our day, the "old religion" is Christianity. True, Christianity is alive and well, and making great strides in Latin America and Africa. But in the United States and Europe, Christianity is largely the unfashionable religion of a bygone era. In the New Testament period Christianity had an advantage: It was a new thing, so many people gave it a hearing.

This need not discourage people, however. Christianity has proved amazingly durable. It is, as one historian noted, "an anvil that has worn out many hammers."

5

Life of the Heart:

DEVOTIONAL READING OF THE BIBLE

In this chapter we will look at several different approaches to studying the Bible. All of them are useful for either beginners or longtime readers. All of them work best if you follow these guidelines:

Learning from the Bible

1. Read regularly.

This seems obvious enough. We exercise regularly, work regular hours at our jobs, watch a favorite TV show at a regular time, eat regularly (oh, yes!), read the newspaper regularly. In short, most important acts in our lives are done regularly. If you plan to get familiar with the Bible, you should count on reading it regularly—and *daily* is the best choice. A time in your day when you can have the fewest distractions is ideal, naturally. This might be just after waking, just before bedtime, during a bus or train commute, during a coffee break—whatever allows you to give the Bible your undivided attention.

2. Set a reasonable goal of time you can commit.

Assuming you can study daily, set a general goal for the amount of time you will read—say, 15 minutes, 20 minutes, whatever you feel is both reasonable and adequate. Anything less than 15 minutes probably won't allow the material to sink in very deeply. If the time commitment seems like a burden, consider the amount of time you spend exercising (for some people, an hour or more a day) or reading mindless periodicals or listening to people talk trash on radio and television. (Don't get the idea that "quality time" with the Bible can mean three quick minutes. Quality is important, but give some thought to quantity, too.)

3. Use a Bible you're comfortable with.

Comfortable here means two things. One, you want a Bible with a typeface you can read easily. A pocket-size Bible can be handy, but if it's hard to read, you probably won't read it. Two, you want a translation you can easily understand. (See pages 63-64 for a discussion of some good contemporary translations.)

4. Learn to underline.

Many people (including myself) are firm believers in underlining. I believe that your most basic tool in Bible study is an underliner—either a regular pen or, even better, a colored marker intended for this purpose. You can underline for different reasons. A passage or verse may inspire you, puzzle you, even irritate you. You might choose to mark passages in different colors—yellow for verses that inspire you, green for those that puzzle you, etc. The point is, underlining lets you interact with the Bible. As you study more, you'll find yourself coming back to places you've underlined and re-experiencing the glow you felt when you first underlined, or perhaps pausing to think about why that passage impressed you at an earlier time.

5. Take notes.

Let's not underestimate the hand-brain connection. Many people can study material closely and absorb it all without ever writing anything down. But most of us can't. The fact is, "putting it in writing" is good for us, mentally speaking. Reading a Bible passage and asking yourself, How do I respond to this? is good.

Writing your response to that question is even better. Writing has a way of clarifying. Thoughts can be vague, shapeless, badly defined. Put on paper, they make more sense. Or, to put it another way, if our thoughts are poorly defined, putting them on paper will make us see just how poorly defined they are.

> "The Bible is alive, it speaks to me; it has feet, it runs after me; it has hands, it lays hold on me."
>
> MARTIN LUTHER,
> REFORMATION LEADER
> (1483–1546)

A technological note: Not everyone has access to a computer, so in this book I never assume that you do. But I also don't assume you *don't* have one. So when I say, "Take notes," this can mean either the old method (pen and paper) or the new method (your fingers on a computer keyboard). The computer has been delightfully liberating for people (including me) whose handwriting is so atrocious that writing notes may be pointless, since we often can't decipher our own scribbling. In front of a computer, many people's fingers can function almost as fast as their brains can. And it's all nice and legible. A resounding "Hallelujah!" for the advancement of computer technology. If you're so inclined, use your computer. It can make note taking on the Bible and your own spiritual life a pleasant experience.

6. Don't be afraid to ask questions.

No one is an expert about every subject. You aren't an expert in the Bible (or you probably wouldn't be reading this book). One nice thing about studying the Bible is that it levels the playing field: A physicist with a Ph.D. may know as little (or as much) about the Bible as a clerk in a shoe store. So don't feel discouraged if you need help.

Don't be afraid to avail yourself of Bible dictionaries and other helps. You'll find these explained in the chapter "Tools for the Bible Reader," pages 231-240.

Don't be afraid to call on a friend, either. If you know someone who seems very much "at home" with the Bible, he or she may be able to help answer the questions you have.

Studying the Bible

Approach 1: A Single Book

The 66 books of the Bible range in the length from one chapter (such as Obadiah, Philemon, Jude, and others) to the very long book of Psalms. Most of the books can be read through in one sitting. This is one way to approach the Bible if you're new to it, or maybe becoming reacquainted with it.

Since Christians see Jesus as the key figure of the Bible, it makes sense to start with one of the four Gospels, the four New Testament books that tell Jesus' story. These are not full-length biographies—certainly not as long as modern-day book-length biographies of famous people. Any of the four Gospels can be read in one sitting of two hours or less. Let's say you want to start with the first Gospel, Matthew.

Read it through. Simply put, read the whole book from beginning to end, without writing anything down and without consulting any reference books. The biggest "snag" you might run into is at the very beginning: Jesus' genealogy, which traces his ancestry from the Hebrew patriarch Abraham. The genealogy runs from Matthew 1:1 to 1:17. Breeze through this long list of names, then slow down when the story starts at 1:18. This is familiar turf: the Christmas story, with Mary, Joseph, the wise men, the star of Bethlehem. For the rest of the book you'll read about Jesus as a teacher and miracle-worker. The main segment of teaching is chapters 5–7, known as the Sermon on the Mount. As you read this section, you'll probably note that some of these wise sayings sound familiar. Toward the end of the Gospel of Matthew, it becomes clear that Jesus is facing opposition. He riles up the Jewish religious establishment, and they, in cahoots with the Roman Empire's government officials, arrange to have Jesus executed by crucifixion. Later he is buried, then miraculously raised to life. He then commissions his followers to preach his message to the whole world.

Again, with this first reading, don't write anything down. That can be done in a later step. But do take some mental notes. Ask yourself these questions:

- What are the main themes here?

- Who are the main characters?

- What words or phrases crop up again and again in the book?

- What does the book teach about morals and behavior?

- What does the book communicate about the nature of God?

- What is your immediate, gut-level response to the book?

> "We ought to listen to the Scriptures with the greatest caution, for as far as our understanding of them goes, we are like little children."
>
> AUGUSTINE, A THEOLOGIAN (354–430)

Read it again, with pen in hand. This step doesn't have to follow immediately after the first reading. But don't wait too long, or you may forget much of what you just read. Try to time the second reading to within 72 hours of the first one.

This time, read the book with a notepad and pen handy. As you read, take time to pause and answer the questions listed above. Also write down:

- chapter and verse numbers of sections you don't understand

- words and names you don't understand

- chapter and verse numbers of sections you find particularly impressive

- chapter and verse numbers of sections you are skeptical about

This second reading should take a good bit longer than the first. You might not even finish it in one sitting. In this reading you can pause, move back and forth from your notes to the text, and flip back and forth between the chapters in Matthew.

Review your notes and write an outline of the book. Have your Bible open to Matthew, but focus on your notes. What have you learned after two readings of the Gospel of Matthew? If your notes list the main themes of Matthew, its main characters, its key words and phrases, its moral teachings, and its view of God, well, then you're way ahead of where you were when you started. If you wrote down which sections impressed you, you might reread those sections.

Then do an outline of the book. This doesn't have to be as neat and organized as an outline you might do for a term paper. But, with your notes and the Gospel of Matthew open in front of you, write down a rough outline of the book's content. Write it as if you were doing a table of contents for the book so that another person could read your outline and get a good idea of what Matthew contains.

If your Bible has study notes, read the notes on Matthew. Some Bibles are straight Bible text and nothing more. But most have some form of notes and study aids. At the bare minimum, most have a few introductory paragraphs at the beginning of Matthew, plus footnotes that explain certain passages. (See pages 22-26 for an explanation of the different types of Bible footnotes.) If your Bible has notes, read through the notes on Matthew, taking time to read the notes and any introductory paragraphs. These study aids are not the Bible itself, and they aren't sacred or holy in the same way as the Bible verses themselves. But the notes and other study aids in most Bibles are reliable and helpful. Chances are they will help answer any questions you had during your second reading. If you find those questions answered, write the answers in your notepad.

If your Bible has no study notes, consult a Bible dictionary or a one-volume Bible commentary. In your notes you wrote down chapter and verse numbers of sections that you didn't understand, or names and terms that puzzled you. You can look up the names and terms in a handy-size Bible dictionary (*Young's Bible Dictionary* from Tyndale House is a good choice). For explanations about sections of Matthew that puzzled you, go to a one-volume Bible commentary. A good commentary can usually explain passages that might puzzle readers.

Let's take an example. Matthew 6:22-23 says, "The eye is the lamp of the body. If your eyes are good, your whole body will be full of light. But if your eyes are bad, your whole body will be full of darkness. If then the light within you is darkness, how great is that darkness!" These are Jesus' words. What do they mean? Even longtime Bible readers puzzle over this passage. In fact, the scholars aren't 100 percent sure of this passage's meaning. It isn't, we gather, concerned with any physical eye problem that an optometrist would treat. Different commentaries give different explanations, yet it's hard to know with certainty what

> "You can learn more about human nature by reading the Bible than by living in New York."
>
> WILLIAM LYON PHELPS, AMERICAN LITERARY CRITIC (1865–1943)

these words mean. This is a case of the "fish bone" problem we discussed on pages 100-103—this is something you can't "eat," so you'll want to push it to the side of the plate for the time being. Matthew 6:22-23 occurs in the middle of a long section that most people find simple and straightforward. So don't hesitate to push Matthew 6:22-23 to the "side of the plate." Don't let your puzzlement over a few passages keep you from enjoying the rest of the book.

(Consider an analogy here: You're reading a Tom Clancy novel and you come to a paragraph with a lot of techno-jargon in it. Maybe you don't understand it all, but chances are you keep reading and enjoying the parts you *do* understand.)

Let's take another example: the term *Pharisees.* Matthew's Gospel says a lot about these people, particularly in chapter 23. If you're not sure you understand just who they were, or if you want to know more about them, you could look up *Pharisees* in a Bible dictionary.

Read the book a third time, focusing on how to apply it to your own life. The first two readings were "get acquainted" times. Now you can get more serious, more in-depth. Keep in mind that the Bible is never about someone else. It is always directed at whoever reads it. It always confronts the reader—not with a threat, but with the question, How do you respond to all this? A related question is, How does this book apply to your current circumstances? After a third reading of Matthew, you could...

- admire Jesus' ethical teaching, believing you should apply it to your own life and attempt to do so
- express awe (or doubts) in response to Jesus' miracles, resulting in a deeper appreciation of divine power, or in doubts about it
- express awe (or doubts) about Jesus' resurrection, resulting in a deeper conviction that Jesus was the Son of God, or in doubts about it
- commit yourself to focus not just on appearing religious outwardly, but being right on the inside—a key theme of Matthew.

Try to memorize a key verse that impressed you. Matthew's Gospel is extremely quotable, so it overflows with verses that stick in the mind. You might choose, for example, "Come to me, all you who are weary and burdened, and I will give you rest" (11:28). Memorize this passage (writing it down a few times always helps), along with the chapter and verse number. For the next week, repeat it to yourself at regular intervals—perhaps after breakfast, or just before going to sleep.

What you've just read is an uncomplicated method to study one book of the Bible. This method will not turn you into a scholar or expert. It will, however, ensure that you are familiar with at least one book of the Bible.

You could work through all the steps above not just with Matthew but with any book of the Bible. If you're fairly new to the Bible, I recommend, after Matthew, the following books:

New Testament

Acts	1 Corinthians
Luke	Ephesians
John	1 Peter
Mark	1 John
James	Hebrews
Romans	

Any of the New Testament books can be read with profit. The ones listed here are generally the easiest to grasp. The sequence they are listed in is deliberate—that is, most people find Acts easier to grasp than the last book in the list, Hebrews. I generally recommend that people avoid the last New Testament book, Revelation, until they are more familiar with the Bible.

Old Testament

Genesis	Daniel (chapters 1–6)
Exodus	Hosea
Psalms	Amos
Proverbs	Micah
Job	Jonah
1 and 2 Samuel	Isaiah
1 and 2 Kings	Jeremiah

You don't have to read the entire New Testament before studying the Old, but I recommend, with the single-book approach, that you read at least three New Testament books before moving on to the Old Testament. The sequence of books I've listed here is just a suggestion, based on how most people react to Old Testament books. The easier books to grasp are the first ones listed—that is, Genesis is easier for most readers than Jeremiah. The Old Testament books not listed here are not bad or unreadable; they are just less readable than the ones listed here. Most people who have read the Bible through will assure you that Job is "more rewarding" to read than Leviticus.

On pages 181-230 you will find summaries of each book of the Bible. This might help you decide which book to study.

Here is a special note to readers who may be getting reacquainted with the Bible after a few years of not reading: An excellent place to begin is the book of Acts. It's a good "action" book, one that shows how the new faith (Christianity) spread in a culture much like ours today.

> "The Bible is a book of faith, and a book of doctrine, and a book of morals, and a book of special revelation from God."
>
> DANIEL WEBSTER, AMERICAN STATESMAN (1782–1852)

Approach 2: A Single Passage

A *passage* is a connected unit of the Bible—say, Matthew 5–7, known as Jesus' Sermon on the Mount. Another popular passage is 1 Corinthians 13, the Bible's famous chapter on love. On pages 156-159 you'll find a list of ethical sections of the Bible—Great Stories, Great Passages, Old Testament Highlights, New Testament Highlights, etc. Studying any of these is a good introduction to the Bible's main teachings.

Choose a passage from that list and read it straight through without stopping. Any of them can be read through in 15 minutes or less.

Then read the passage again, slowly, and this time take notes.

- Summarize the passage in a paragraph or two. If the passage tells a story, summarize the story and characters. If the passage contains teaching, summarize the main ideas.

- Give the passage a title. This could be a short summary of the paragraph or two you just wrote. Or you could phrase it in some catchy, clever way—as if you were packaging it to advertise it.

- Write down what the passage seems to say about what God is like. Loving? Just? Holy? Angry at sin? Forgiving?

- Write down what the passage says about human nature.

- Write down any moral commands (if any) that are in the passage. You might quote these exactly, or restate them in your own words.

- Write down any promises from God. Again, you can quote these or restate them in your own words.

- Write down any contemporary situations you think the passage applies to. For example, if you're studying 1 Corinthians 13, the "love chapter," it might strike you that the contemporary divorce rate would be different if married couples remembered these words from the passage: "Love does not delight in evil but rejoices with the truth. It always protects, always trusts, always hopes, always perseveres."

- Write down anything about the passage you don't understand. You can look these up in a Bible dictionary or commentary. If you still don't understand the parts that puzzle you, don't despair. This shouldn't keep you from reading and enjoying the parts you do understand.

If you apply this approach to all the passages listed on pages 156-59 (and this would take a while), then you will gain a very good overview of the high points of the Bible.

Approach 3: A Topic

Is there a topic of great interest to you? Such as divorce, child-rearing, money, heaven and hell, etc. If you knew the Bible by heart, you could immediately call to mind what the Bible says on those subjects. But if that's not the case, then you will want resources that can help you trace a topic through the Bible.

Two study aids that can help you greatly are a concordance and a topical Bible. (See pages 234-35;237 for more about these.) A concordance lists words in alphabetical order, showing where they appear in the Bible. A topical Bible lists in full the passages in which a topic is covered.

Let's say you're interested in what the Bible says about money. You could look up *money* in a topical Bible, and it would show you the most important Bible passages on that subject. It would also refer you to related sections, such as *wealth, riches,* or *possessions.*

You could also look up *money* in a concordance. This would

point you to every Bible verse that contains that word. (You'd have to look up each verse yourself, of course.) To really cover the topic, though, you'd need to look under all the related words as well—again, *wealth, riches, possessions,* and even *gold* and *silver.* If you're really interested in the topic or word, look up each verse listed in the concordance. Write each verse down, or at least the ones that say something significant.

A good Bible dictionary (such as the handy-sized *Young's Bible Dictionary*) can be useful when studying a topic. So can a very useful book called *A Theological Word Book of the Bible* (by A. Richardson, Macmillan Publishers, 1962). In spite of its title, it looks at most topics of interest, not just ones that are theological.

When you've worked your way through all the verses (including the verses with related words like *wealth*), look back through what you've written down. Try to summarize in a paragraph or two what the Bible says as a whole on this topic. If a few of the verses seem to contradict each other, look beyond that and ask, What are most of these verses teaching on the subject?

Then write down what these verses mean in terms of your behavior. In other words, if you take all these verses seriously, what impact will they have (if any) on your behavior? Are there any changes you would or should make? What are they? What effect do these verses have on your attitude toward God? Toward other people? What major changes (if any) have occurred to you as a result of studying this topic?

Many people enjoy the topical approach. One thing you need to beware of is choosing a topic that is too big. Love, for example, is an excellent topic—but it is so broad that you could be looking up verses for days. Narrow down a broad topic. Instead of pursuing the broad topic of love, focus on God's love for us, or our love for God, or love for other people. Each of these is also a broad topic, but they are more manageable than just love in general. One suggestion is to focus on "love of neighbor." Use a concordance to find where *neighbor* occurs in the Bible. You'll find it refers not just to the person living next door, but to people we encounter in life—not always pleasant people, but people that the Bible instructs us to show compassion to anyway.

One other hazard to guard against: Make sure you study your topics in balance with other topics in the Bible. For example, you may choose to study Jesus' sayings about God's love. This is a great topic, one worthy of study. But realize that when you study this, you will want to balance it with its "flip side." No one

> "What you bring away from the Bible depends to some extent on what you carry to it."
>
> OLIVER WENDELL HOLMES,
> AMERICAN AUTHOR
> (1809–1894)

in the Bible said more about God's love than Jesus. But the "flip side" is that Jesus had a lot to say about hell and damnation—the consequence of ignoring God's love. We tend to choose topics we like and feel comfortable with, such as God's love. But if you want a balanced view of the Bible, try choosing a subject that challenges you and makes you uncomfortable—such as judgement, or hell, for example. If you really want to challenge yourself and make yourself uncomfortable, do a study of the unsettling topic "the human tongue and the evils it is capable of." The Bible has a lot to say about this subject, and the subject is still relevant today.

Approach 4: A Single Verse

You could call this "microstudy" of the Bible. It involves study—"up-close and personal"—of a single verse of the Bible.

Of course, this should not be the only approach you use to study the Bible. To know the Bible well, you need to get the big picture, and to get that you need to read through some entire books, as suggested in Approach 1.

A comparison is in order: If you wanted to be an expert on Steven Spielberg movies, you'd want to see all the movies he's directed. Doing that would give you an idea of his approach to moviemaking. And you'd become familiar with the variety of movies he's done. To really get to know his style well, you might concentrate on one of his movies—say, *Raiders of the Lost Ark*. And if you really wanted to study his style in detail, you might pick one scene from *Raiders* and watch it again and again on video, closely observing the camera angles, use of sound, acting, lighting, costumes, the set, etc. This kind of close study is enriching. So is watching all his movies. The two approaches are both rewarding, in different ways.

Well, those who wrote the Bible might feel this analogy is appropriate, but they would quickly tell us that the Bible is more important (and even more interesting) than a Spielberg movie. I agree, or else this book you are holding would never have been written.

Choose a verse. Don't do this at random (for instance, by opening the Bible and pointing your finger at a verse on the page). This method might help you select a good verse for study, or your finger might fall on some law in Leviticus about sacrificing sheep. So choose a verse that you have already read as a result of reading an entire book or a passage (Approaches 1 and 2) or studying a topic (Approach 3).

Let's say you read through the entire first letter of John (known as 1 John for short). This short letter is dense—that is, it's packed full of important teaching about living the Christian life. Let's pick a verse from this letter: "The world and its desires pass away, but the man who does the will of God lives forever" (2:17). This is a good verse to choose because it is understandable and full of meaning.

Read the verse in context. Most Bibles are divided into paragraphs. To get the context of 1 John 2:17, you will want to read the paragraph that contains 2:17 (or even read all of chapter 2). But definitely read the paragraph that contains 2:17. Ask yourself what the meaning of the entire paragraph is. You'll find that 2:17 is part of a paragraph on the subject of loving the world. The paragraph contrasts the love of the world and its pleasures with the love of God the Father. So 2:17 sort of sums up the entire paragraph.

If you have a commentary, look up the verse. A good commentary can give you additional insights into the verse, and perhaps even reveal the meaning of the original languages. You don't have to know Hebrew and Greek to enjoy and understand the Bible. But be glad that Bible scholars are able to explain some of the meanings of Greek and Hebrew words that don't always come through in the English translations.

If the verse has footnotes that refer you to other Bible verses, read them. This verse, 1 John 2:17, doesn't have any. Lots of Bible verses do. In the New Testament, many verses have footnotes indicating that the verse is quoting or referring to an Old Testament verse. For example, 1 John 3:12, which mentions Cain and Abel, has a footnote that reads "Genesis 4:8." That footnote refers you to the part of Genesis where Cain, Adam and Eve's son, murdered his brother Abel. You might already be familiar with that story. If not, the footnote referring you to Genesis 4:8 helps point you to that account.

Rewrite the verse in your own words. Try to restate the verse without using many of the words in the verse. You might restate it by personalizing it. For example: "If I am obedient to the Lord, I live eternally. And the things around me, the things people pursue, aren't made to last."

Apply the verse to your life. First John 2:17 could have several applications:

1. Remember that I am made to live eternally.
2. Subordinating my will to God's will is critical.
3. The things in the world that seem so attractive aren't made to last.

Approach 5: Biography

Would you rather read a biography or a book of theology? Most people would quickly pick a biography. Thankfully, the Bible contains a lot of biographies. In fact, it offers a lot of both. Instead of giving its theology in the form of dry propositions, it gives theology-in-action—that is, you learn about God and man by watching God interacting with people.

The key person for study is, of course, Jesus. His four brief biographies in the New Testament are known as the Gospels. You can, and should, study all four of them.

But the Bible abounds with fascinating people, and it has no hesitancy about showing them "warts and all." Except for Jesus himself, there are no superheroes in the Bible. Heroes, yes—but these heroes all have flaws and weaknesses, which makes them more interesting and reminds us again and again that we ought to worship God, not human beings.

If you choose to study a particular person, you will need a concordance. This will show you where to find all the Bible passages about that person. Or, for the people listed below, you can read the Bible passages given in the parentheses.

Some obvious choices for study:

Paul the apostle (Acts 7:58–8:1-3; 9:1-31; 13–28; 1 Corinthians 16; 2 Corinthians 6; 10–12; Philippians 1:12-30; 2:19-29; 3:1-11; 2 Timothy 4:9-22; Philemon). In Acts, Paul is the chief character. Combining Acts with some personal passages from Paul's letters, we have a vivid portrait of this fascinating man of faith who was a missionary, pastor, and theologian.

David (1 Samuel 16–1 Kings 2:12). No Old Testament man's life is shown in more vivid detail than David's. We see him as shepherd boy, giant-killer, musician and poet, warrior, king, bosom friend, husband, adulterer, father, subject of a conspiracy, old man. Most importantly, he is shown as a man of deep and exuberant faith.

Samuel (1 Samuel 1–10; 12–13; 15–16; 25:1,28). Samuel is prophet, judge, and kingmaker. His story intertwines with those of David and Saul.

Saul (1 Samuel 8–2 Samuel 1). Israel's first king is an inspiring but tragic figure. You could easily spend a long time studying Samuel, Saul, and David together.

Abraham (Genesis 12–25). The "father of the faithful," Abraham is a great role model in spite of his noted character flaws. The Israelites looked upon Abraham as the nation's true spiritual father. Study him and find out why.

Jacob and his 12 sons (Genesis 27–50). Jacob, also named Israel, is both cunning trickster and man of God. His relations with his twin brother, Esau, are sometimes amusing, sometimes touching.

His favoritism toward one particular son is an object lesson in how *not* to handle one's children.

Joseph (Genesis 37; 39–50). Joseph is the most interesting of Jacob's 12 sons and the best role model. Some parts of his tale are heart-wrenching. The story never grows old, as proven by the popularity of the musical *Joseph and the Amazing Technicolor Dreamcoat*.

> "The devil can cite Scripture for his purpose."
>
> WILLIAM SHAKESPEARE

Moses (Exodus 1–20; 32–34; Numbers 10:11–14:45; 16:1–17:13; 20–25; Deuteronomy 34). As proven by the ever-popular movie *The Ten Commandments,* Moses' story is not boring. Israel's liberator and lawgiver is one of the most important Old Testament figures (other than God, that is).

Gideon (Judges 6–8). The great judge (champion) of Israel makes a good short study, given that his life story occupies only three chapters in Judges.

Samson (Judges 13–16). The Israelite strongman is both hulk and man of God. Samson and the wily Delilah are known even by people who have never opened a Bible.

Ruth (the book of Ruth, naturally). This sweet story touches everyone who reads it. Ruth is a great role model of faith and womanly devotion.

Solomon (1 Kings 1–11). Son of David and Israel's "golden boy," Solomon is both majestic and, at the end, tragic. Find out why he became the symbol of both wisdom and luxury in Israel.

Elijah (1 Kings 17–19, 21; 2 Kings 1–2). The fiery prophet of the Lord is preacher, miracle-worker, and scolder of the mighty. His confrontations with wicked Queen Jezebel are fascinating.

Elisha (1 Kings 19:16-21; 2 Kings 2–9:13; 13:14-21). Elijah's successor is another miracle-worker and confronter of kings.

Hezekiah (2 Kings 18–20). A rarity: a highly moral king of Israel! His story intertwines with that of the prophet Isaiah.

Josiah (2 Kings 22:1–23:29). Israel's last king with any moral fiber. He is not only a king but a reformer, one who meets a tragic end.

Stephen (Acts 6–7). The first martyr for the Christian faith, and an eloquent speaker to boot. His final speech to an angry mob makes for good reading.

Peter (Acts 1–5; 9:32–12:19; 15:1-21). The most interesting of Jesus' 12 disciples. Before you study his life in Acts, become familiar with how he is presented in the Gospels.

The Bible is never content to record raw history. It draws morals so you don't have to guess at why certain life stories were included. But as you study the lives of these people, jot down your answers to these questions:

- What are this person's chief virtues?

- What are his chief weaknesses?

- How does my own life resemble this person's?

- Is my own life moving in a good (or bad) direction that is similar to this person's life? Can that direction be changed? How?

- What key verse or passage from this person's story is worth memorizing? (You might choose one that in some way summarizes the person's character.)

- What is the one incident in the person's story that sticks in your mind? (This could be something that shows him at his best or worst.)

Approach 6: From Beginning to End

My feeling about this approach can be summed up in one word: *Don't.* This was a common practice in my grandmother's generation. She readily admits that this practice often became more of a duty than a pleasure.

This approach seems neat and tidy. If you follow it, you will eventually have read the entire Bible—every word of it. That's good, but if you begin at Genesis 1 and try to get all the way to Revelation, you might not make it. Not many people do, for this requires great discipline.

An alternative is to try *The One-Year Bible,* published by Tyndale House. This is available in several translations, including the New International Version. It neatly divides the Bible into 365 readings, one for each day of the year. (You can take a break on February 29 in Leap Year, obviously.) *The One-Year Bible* begins on January 1 with the beginning of the Old Testament (Genesis 1) and the New (Matthew 1), plus a selection from Psalms and Proverbs. The beauty of this is that when you're working through some of the more difficult parts of the Old Testament (say, Leviticus, Numbers, 1 Chronicles), you'll still have a more meaningful New Testament reading each day. Another popular volume that also divides the Bible in 365 readings is Harvest House's *NIV Daily Bible.*

> "Nobody ever outgrows Scripture; the Book widens and deepens with our years."
>
> C.H. SPURGEON,
> FAMOUS PREACHER IN
> VICTORIAN ENGLAND
> (1834–1892)

If you read the Bible straight through, even if you're using *The One-Year Bible,* you may want to turn to pages 181-230 of this book and refer to the summaries of the Bible's books as a guide.

Approach 7: A Contemporary Issue

This approach to Bible study can be very rewarding. It will also involve more effort on your part. Many contemporary topics—marriage, money, children, for example—can be studied through Approach 3. This approach is similar, but has to do with important issues of concern to people today. You might also check to see if your local Christian bookstore has a Bible-based study guide to the particular contemporary issue that is of interest to you.

Approach 8: Alternate Between the Other Seven Approaches

Of the eight approaches above, is there a "best"? Yes—any of them is best compared to the usual approach of many people, which is not studying the Bible at all. And no, none of the eight is better than the other seven. All eight have their advantages and disadvantages. But all eight will get you deeper into the Bible.

The Family Plan

All the approaches mentioned above are suitable for your individual use. All are also suitable for a group. But studying with your family is another matter. In fact, if you take the Bible seriously, you should do it.

For couples without kids

If your spouse has no interest in studying the Bible, don't try to force it. Marriages are difficult enough without deliberately introducing conflict. On the other hand, do at least bring up the possibility of studying as a couple. You might be surprised by the answer you get.

"Hon, this may sound crazy, but I'm thinking about studying the Bible for a few minutes each day."

There are several possible responses to this:

"Fine."

"Hrmph."

"So what?"

"What a waste of time. Don't expect me to get involved!"

"Why?"

Yet one additional possible response is, "Really? I think that might be interesting."

Scheduling a regular time of study for yourself can be a challenge. Setting aside time for two can be even more of a challenge. But given that the Bible is such a special book, this is a commitment worth making.

Again, you can use any of the eight approaches described above. But as a couple, you can introduce some other elements:

1. Read to each other. That is, one reads while the other listens.

You could take turns reading on alternate days. The listener can also be the "note taker."

2. Answer the questions described in the Approach sections above, but discuss them together. You will probably agree and disagree. One spouse may see something the other didn't.

3. Discuss how the text you're studying applies to your marriage (if indeed it does). If you're studying alone, this is a good question to ask yourself, also. But you can certainly have some interesting discussion with your spouse about how the Bible applies to the two of you as a couple.

If the two of you are interested in using the topical method (Approach 3), one logical topic to study is *marriage*, while another is *men and women*. The Bible has a lot to say about both these topics.

One other suggestion if you study the Bible with your spouse: Be honest with each other about how you react to the text. In a group Bible study, a person is often reluctant to say, "This passage is offensive!" or "Oh, come on!" or "I don't grasp this at all!" With your spouse, you don't have to appear pious or wise. The Bible has been around for centuries, so there's nothing you can say about it that hasn't been said before, no criticism that someone else hasn't said already. Don't expect that every sentence in the Bible will be understandable, or that it will square with your own beliefs about God and human behavior. Be willing to wrestle with the Bible—and be willing to change your opinions, too. (You might want to reread the section on the Bible's "fish bones" on pages 100-103.)

Bringing the kids on board

Children have a built-in advantage over adults: They don't approach the Bible with any prior assumptions, thinking that it's dull, boring, or old-fashioned. So they can do something that too many adults don't allow themselves to do: enjoy it, get lost in it, frolic in the good stories in it. Kids can enjoy Samson, Noah, David,

Paul, Moses, and, yes, Jesus. They might have difficulty with the long teaching passages in Paul's letters or the laws in parts of the Old Testament. But kids enjoy—and learn—through stories.

A question arises here: Doesn't the Bible contain violence and sex? Yes, it does. A book whose central character dies on a cross with nails through his wrists is not, I admit, shy about violence. The violence is there—wars, murders, executions, child sacrifice, you name it. Sex is there, too—adultery, prostitution, homosexuality, the whole nine yards. (Mark Twain snickered that some libraries banned his "scandalous" books while they kept the Bible on their shelves. It's true that the Bible is more graphic than *Huckleberry Finn.*)

Well, parents are right to be concerned about their kids' exposure to violence and sex. Television and movies are already a problem. But the violence and sex in the Bible is radically different. In the Bible, sex is not romanticized, unless you count the Song of Solomon. The Bible presents marriage as the only moral option. Sex outside marriage is bad—as vividly portrayed in David's adultery with Bathsheba, in the shocking story of the homosexual men of Sodom, in the painful tale of Absalom raping his half-sister, Tamar. Unlike TV sitcoms, the Bible doesn't snicker at immorality. It is never treated as something to amuse people. So the Bible's frankness about sex is a good antidote to the usual immorality in the media. One word of warning: The Old Testament does seem to take polygamy in stride. The Israelite men who had more than one wife (or concubine) were not condemned for this practice. The New Testament, however, presents the one-spouse situation as normal (and, incidentally, has a strict view of divorce).

You'll have to judge your kids' capacity to deal with sexual matters. The older they are, obviously, the franker you can be. But even with very small children (who probably can't grasp the physical meaning of adultery) you can point out the Bible's emphasis on marital fidelity.

As for violence, the Bible is a good antidote to the images of violence in the media. Television and movies make violence look like a game. By contrast, the Bible shows violence as horrible, not entertaining. Some parts (notably the books of Joshua and Judges) present the troubling picture of God's nation, Israel, slaughtering other people. But generally the Bible, particularly the New Testament, teaches a love ethic that has no place for physical cruelty. A key point: Jesus was the victim of violence, but he made it clear that his followers could not strike back with violence.

If your kids are 12 or under, you may not be able to use all the study approaches mentioned earlier. Since kids are interested in stories and characters, you may want to focus on a character (Approach 5) or on a single book (Approach 1) if the book has enough action (the Gospels, Acts, 1 and 2 Samuel). You can use all the discussion questions described above but may need to simplify them for your children.

> "The greatest source of material for motion pictures is the Bible, and almost any chapter would serve as a basic idea for a motion picture."
>
> CECIL B. DEMILLE,
> MOVIE DIRECTOR,
> FAMOUS FOR
> THE TEN COMMANDMENTS

Another option is for you and your spouse to pursue one Bible study plan while you do another with your kids. These could be totally different, or the same. For example, let's say you are studying the book of 1 Samuel. You study separately for 20 minutes per day. Then, with your children, read to them from a Bible story book about Samuel, Saul, or David. Since you're studying those characters yourself, there's no harm in reinforcing your learning by sharing these stories with the kids. In fact, as all teachers know, there's a lot to be said for retelling a story to kids. It helps you to use your imagination. Instead of just reading through a story (say, David and Goliath, or Daniel in the lions' den) without giving much thought to it, retelling the story to your kids encourages you to visualize it, dramatize it, focus on some visual details, verbalize what the characters' thoughts and feelings were. Retelling a story for kids also helps you figure out the key points about it. What's important here? What's the bottom line? "Dumbing down" a Bible story isn't a bad thing—it means you're making a story simple enough and clear enough for a child to understand. Generations of people who were exposed to the Bible as children prove that this can have a very positive effect.

A bookstore can supply you with Bible storybooks for children of every age. These are good—especially if you're not too familiar with the Bible yourself. (There's also a well-kept secret about Bible storybooks for kids: Because they present their material simply and directly, they're often more appealing to adults than guides written for adults.)

Don't pass up a chance to have fun with your kids and exercise your own mind and imagination at the same time. If your kids are willing, share a Bible story time together, with you (or you and your spouse together) as both storyteller and actor. Have fun doing this—parents sometimes forget that they themselves can amuse their own kids. You can have a good time, bond with your kids, reinforce your own learning of the Bible, and teach some good moral lessons.

The earlier you start doing this with your children, the better. Teach them that the Bible is user-friendly. It can be enjoyed, it can teach life lessons, and it can be shared by the whole family. It does not have to be just a "church book."

The teen factor

If you have children above age 14—or if you are a teen yourself—any of the study approaches mentioned earlier will work. A teen who willingly engages in Bible reading with his family is… well, remarkable. A teen who chooses to study the Bible on his own is probably more common. At the age when the teen is "finding himself," the desire to study the Bible alone is something you should encourage, not discourage.

Sometimes as children grow older, they may try to opt out of family Bible time. This doesn't mean they've forever turned against the Bible. It may be they aren't interested for the time being. Don't force them to read the Bible. Rather, let them see you studyng it, enjoying it, even living by its teachings. If you have exposed your children to the Bible in early childhood, you have done all you can do. Perhaps they will eventually return to reading the Bible, or be encouraged to do so when they see your example.

READ-ALOUD TIME?

In the ancient world, reading always meant reading *aloud*—never silently to oneself. People just assumed that the written word had to be "brought to life" by speech. In our own day, a subway car might be filled with readers, each person reading to himself silently. This wouldn't have happened in Bible times. A scroll—the ancient version of books—was a public, not private, message. It was intended to be shared. There was a community feeling about literature. Only a few rich people had private libraries, so most of the scrolls that circulated were shared. In other words, it was highly unusual for one person to read the Bible by himself. Frequently, others were within hearing distance.

6

Yes? No? Maybe?

DECISION MAKING AND THE BIBLE

. . . .

Should I marry Chris?"

"Should I have an abortion?"

"Should I take the kids to Disney World or the mountains?"

"Should I wear my blue or gray suit today?"

"Should I return this wallet I found to its owner?"

"Should I stay with my old job or look for a new one?"

"Should I have waffles or pancakes for breakfast?"

"Should I... ?" Every day you make decisions, which means you make choices—some of which are moral choices, and others which are mere matters of taste. Some of them are major, and others are minor. Some can affect your whole future, while others will have no effect beyond the next five minutes.

This is the way God designed us—so the Bible tells us. He made us free, capable of choosing the good or the bad. Under the name of *sin* are the bad choices, the things that (according to God) are bad for us. The Bible never assumes that you will escape making bad choices. In fact, the only person presented as sinless in the Bible is Jesus. Everyone else—even great heroes such as David and Moses— made bad choices. That's the bad news. The good news is that God is always willing to forgive. The other good news is that we can be guided so that we maker fewer mistakes. This is a combination that attracts many people to the Bible: a forgiving God, plus moral guidance. In other words, the Bible offers us guidance to keep us from failing, and it reveals to us a God who forgives our failures.

Of course, if you want guidance in life, you don't have to go to the Bible. Guidance is easy to find elsewhere. The bookstore shelves are bulging with books about taking control of your own life. The airwaves are also full of such advice. Psychologists and other self-appointed experts pour out their free advice via radio every day. Some of their advice may seem sound, and some of it is ridiculous. The same goes for the advice of friends, co-workers, and family members. Many people are eager to give advice (even if their own lives are a shambles). If you're wise, you probably take most of it with a grain of salt. But the world is so confusing and so full of choices that most of us do feel a powerful urge to get help of some kind.

If you're reading this chapter, I'll assume you believe the Bible can give us moral guidance. In all the history of Christianity (and Judaism, also), believers have assumed that the Bible was more than a book of history or theology. They believed (and still do) that the Bible shows us what God wants for human life. They believed that God's will for us is not that we be strangled by thousands of rules, but that we have some plain, basic guidelines that can help make us better human beings.

Ways People Use the Bible in Decision Making

There are several ways to approach the Bible as a resource for decision making.

1. The Bible has commandments for leading a moral life.

Some people like to emphasize the parts of the Bible that have clear-cut moral commands. The Ten Commandments are an example: "You shall not murder. You shall not commit adultery. You shall not steal" (Exodus 20:13-15). It is quite clear that some behaviors are definitely prohibited by the Bible. Where it speaks clearly, there is no argument. You cannot steal your neighbor's lawn mower

Bibliomancy is the name given to the practice of opening the Bible and reading a passage at random. Some people do this when they're looking for guidance in life. This is not recommended. After all, a person considering suicide might open the Bible to the passage that says Judas "went away and hanged himself" (Matthew 27:5).

and hope that you'll find a passage in the Bible that will condone what you did. On some issues the Bible is refreshingly clear.

The problem is, the Bible doesn't issue direct commandments about everything. A married man knows that the Bible commands him not to cheat on his wife. But does it forbid him from paging through a porn magazine? In terms of direct commandments, no, it doesn't. The Bible makes it clear that we shouldn't engage in cheating and swindling on the job. But it gives no command regarding changing careers, or how to know if a particular job is right for us. We are told not to murder, which is clear enough. But what if someone attacks your spouse or children and you kill that person? Commandments are simple; life is complex.

2. The Bible gives us moral direction by showing us role models of faith.

The Bible includes many accounts of the lives of faithful men and women. By studying the words and acts of Moses, Paul, David, Ruth, and, above all, Jesus himself, we can learn about moral responsibility and the life of faith. Rather than just focusing on rules, we can focus on people who embody the moral life.

Role models can work in reverse, too. King David is shown as being, generally, a good man, a real man of God. But his moral failures are depicted in painful detail in the Bible. We see David "warts and all"—David the loyal friend, the joyous lover of God, the forgiving king, but also David the adulterer, the overindulgent father, the all-too-human human. We can learn a lot by reading about David's forgiveness toward his enemy Saul (1 Samuel 24) as well as about his adultery with Bathsheba (2 Samuel 11–12). Morally, David shows us what to do and what to avoid.

One problem we face today is that some of our circumstances do not correspond to any faced by the people in the Bible. Many of their problems are similar to ours, but not all of them. The issue of abortion, for example, is not addressed directly in the Bible.

3. The Bible's moral guidance comes to us when we focus on God.

The Bible tells us a lot about God. He is Creator of everything, the Savior who rescues us from our selfishness and sins, and the Spirit who lives within our hearts and consciences to guide us daily. Beyond focusing on rules or on role models of faith, we can also focus on God himself. When we know more about him, we have a clearer idea of how he wishes for us to live. As we read the Bible, we see that God is holy, just, merciful, forgiving, caring. He wants our freely given love and fellowship.

What's more, the Bible tells us to imitate God: "Be imitators of God, therefore, as dearly loved children" (Ephesians 5:1). To imitate God, we have to know what he is like. We learn more about him by reading the Bible, and also by getting to know him "up close and personal."

The Bible has a lot to say about *loving* God. This is one thing that sets the Bible's religion apart from most other world religions. We are, according to the Bible, supposed to love God because… well, mainly because God is God, the great Being who made us and cares about us. You won't find that kind of love for a god expressed in other ancient writings. You can read all the great literature by the Greeks and Romans, but you won't find anything about genuine love for the gods Zeus or Mars or Athena. You'll find fear, respect, and admiration, but not love. This is something unique about the God of the Bible: He wants people to love him of their own free will.

4. The Bible teaches us to love.

Jesus proclaimed that there were really only two commandments: " 'Love the Lord your God with all your heart and with all your soul and with all your strength and with all your mind' and, 'Love your neighbor as yourself' " (Luke 10:27). He also told his followers, "A new command I give you: Love one another. As I have loved you, so you must love one another" (John 13:34). Doesn't this sound much better (and perhaps easier) than following a set of rules? The whole New Testament emphasizes this theme: Love is more important than rules.

There is one problem, however: Love (as the Bible pictures it) is more than just warm, fuzzy feelings. Love for others and for God may involve self-denial. It may lead us to do things that go against our natural instincts. As wonderful as love sounds, the self-giving love that the Bible talks about is far different from the love spoken of in pop songs and movies. Paul's description of love in 1 Corinthians 13 is radically different from the selfish "love" in Top 40 songs. It is clear in the Bible that *love* is not a synonym for temporary lust. It is clear that love doesn't necessarily involve physical attraction to a person or even liking him very much. It involves seeking his welfare, not just satisfying our urges. Most of us learn about this kind of love in our families, where we often get angry or irritated with our parents, siblings, and children. Though we might not really *like* our relatives, we know we're to love them.

> "This great Book is the best gift God has given to man. But for it, we could not know right from wrong."
>
> ABRAHAM LINCOLN,
> SIXTEENTH U.S. PRESIDENT

Real love is the warm, human side of commandments. Love turns the negative *Don't* into a positive *Do.*

These are four ways people can view the Bible. Actually, a person can hold more than one view—perhaps even all four. All are valid. We should know the Bible's direct commandments. We should know its stories of people of faith. We should know how it portrays the character of God. And we should know what it says about love (including the ways that real love differs from love as most people define it).

Ten Rules of Thumb When You're Looking for Guidance

1. Learn the Bible's direct commands.

God's commands are practical and cover a lot of life's situations. The fundamental ones are in the Ten Commandments (Exodus 20). These basic morals include respect for others' property ("You shall not steal"), for honesty ("You shall not give false testimony against your neighbor"), for marriage and sexual morality ("You shall not commit adultery"), reverence for human life ("You shall not murder"), respect for authority ("Honor your father and your mother"). These are so basic that most people would agree on them even if they weren't in the Bible. Most people know instinctively that they shouldn't cheat on their spouse, lie about a fellow worker, verbally abuse a parent, or kill someone. Most of people's moral decisions are, if they thought about it, pretty clear-cut. Should you cheat on your income tax? No, that's stealing (even if you are irked at how the government spends your money). Should you have an extramarital affair? No, that's adultery, even if your spouse does get on your nerves sometimes.

Interestingly, the Ten Commandments also include, "You shall have no other gods," "You shall not make for yourself an idol," and "You shall not covet." Most people won't see how these apply to life today. Ah, but they do. The first one ("You shall have no other gods") means we aren't supposed to worship anything except the true God. Do we? Of course. People worship many things—their careers, their homes, their status, their own gratification, even their own bodies (or someone else's). The second commandment is similar: "You shall not make for yourself an idol." People do, however—everything from clothing to home decor to the airbrushed images in men's magazines. The Bible makes it clear: This is wrong. Not only do the Ten Commandments forbid the idolizing of things around us, but the whole history of Israel is a story of a nation that forgot the true God and worshipped something else.

What about the command, "You shall not covet"? Here is a direct command that concerns our hearts rather than our actions. We may be able to conceal our envy of other people, but God knows our thoughts. This commandment lets us know that even if we look moral on the outside, we can still be wrong on the inside.

At the end of this chapter you'll find a list of the key "command" passages in the Bible. These do not (to many people's surprise) make up a very large part of the Bible. If you think the whole Bible is nothing more than a rule book, you may be pleasantly surprised.

By the way, you'll feel better about the Bible's commands if you know what they were designed for: to help you lead a happy, constructive life. God, who is a Father, didn't issue his decrees just to keep us from having fun or to show us he's the Boss. The rules are there for the same reason all good rules exist: to make life better. Most of us dislike the speed limits on interstate highways. (And we especially dislike it when we're caught breaking the limit.) But we'll usually admit, if we're pressed, that the limits serve a purpose: getting us (and other people) where we're going in relative safety. As with most rules, we sincerely believe that other people should obey the rules, even if we ourselves grumble about them. After all, why is that guy on the highway in such a hurry? Isn't 65 miles per hour a reasonable speed limit for him? Then it probably is for us, as well.

> "This is the people's book of revelation, revelation of themselves not alone, but revelation of life and of peace."
>
> WOODROW WILSON, TWENTY-EIGHTH U.S. PRESIDENT

2. Learn to apply the direct commands to other situations.

Intelligence, as we all know, is more than just knowing facts. It involves dealing creatively with what happens to us. A kid in an urban ghetto may not be "book smart," but he may learn to use his wits to survive in the city jungle. In the same way, each of us—regardless of how much formal education we have—has a brain that we can use to live intelligently. God has given us our brains. The willingness to use our brain is our own choice.

OLD TESTAMENT
VS. NEW TESTAMENT?

Many people have the impression that the two parts of the Bible are radically different—particularly in their moral teaching. You might have heard that the Old Testament teaches "an eye for an eye," while the New Testament teaches mercy, kindness, and forgiveness.

Well, this is a good reason to study the Old Testament more closely. It's true that some parts of the Old Testament—such as the Psalms, for example—sound vengeful. They call on God to punish Israel's enemies. The idea of getting even is definitely present in the Old Testament. This is natural considering that the nation of Israel was constantly harassed by the powerful nations that surrounded Israel.

But there's more to the Old Testament. Consider these ethical statements:

> Do not hate your brother in your heart. Rebuke your neighbor frankly so you will not share in his guilt. Do not seek revenge or bear a grudge against one of your people, but love your neighbor as yourself. I am the LORD (Leviticus 19:17-18).

> If you come across your enemy's ox or donkey wandering off, be sure to take it back to him. If you see the donkey of someone who hates you fallen down under its load, do not leave it there; be sure you help him with it (Exodus 23:4-5).

> Do not gloat when your enemy falls; when he stumbles, do not let your heart rejoice (Proverbs 24:17).

> If your enemy is hungry, give him food to eat; if he is thirsty, give him water to drink. In doing this, you will heap burning coals on his head, and the LORD will reward you (Proverbs 25:21-22).

This last verse was quoted by Paul, the Christian apostle, in his letter to the Romans (12:20). He was quoting Proverbs, but many people think that Romans 12:20 was an original Christian ethical teaching from the mind of Paul. Many people also believe Jesus was the first to say, "Love your neighbor as yourself." But he was quoting Leviticus 19:18.

The more we read the Old Testament, the more we discover how much of it is quoted in the New Testament.

The brain can absorb rules such as, "You shall not murder" and "You shall not commit adultery." These are understandable. These and the other direct commandments in the Bible would (if people obeyed them) make the world a better place. Society would be better, and individual lives would be better.

But not all moral decisions are covered by the Bible's commandments. What does the Bible say about smoking? About abortion? About nuclear weapons? Not a word. If you don't care to think creatively, you could say, "Well, I looked through the Bible and didn't find a word about pornography, so I guess it's okay to read smutty books." Well, while the Bible doesn't say anything about pornography *directly*, it does say, "You shall not commit adultery." The married man might reply, "Well, I'm not committing adultery. I'm just looking at pictures, and isn't that much better than having an affair?"

It is at this point we should turn to Jesus' Sermon on the Mount (Matthew 5–7). This is one of the key sections on morality in the Bible. In it, Jesus looks at the moral commandments and tells his listeners that they ought to go beyond the obvious meanings of the commands. Consider his words in Matthew 5:27-28: "You have heard that it was said, 'Do not commit adultery.' But I tell you that anyone who looks at a woman lustfully has already committed adultery with her in his heart." Meaning what? The key idea here is that our minds can sin, not just our bodies. Jesus was telling people

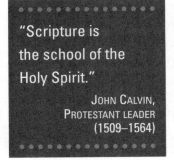

"Scripture is the school of the Holy Spirit."

JOHN CALVIN,
PROTESTANT LEADER
(1509–1564)

to avoid not only literal adultery, but also adultery in the mind. In other words, you can be unfaithful from the neck up. And most people know, deep down, when an appreciative look at an attractive person has progressed into physical lust.

So does this apply to pornography? Probably. Certainly the Bible makes it clear that a married person has no business viewing magazines or videos that lead to mental unfaithfulness. What about an unmarried person? Let's look at that next.

3. Learn about the type of life the Bible intends us to live.

It bears repeating that the rules in the Bible aren't there to deny us pleasure, but to keep us from harm and to make us better people. Good parents make rules for their children to protect them, and God is the same way.

So the Bible gives us more than just rules. It gives us pictures of what the good life is like. We see the good life portrayed in the lives of certain individuals—most notably Jesus. What did Jesus do? He healed the sick, raised the dead, showed forgiveness to enemies, showed love to both rich and poor, didn't gossip or slander, showed little concern for material things, and gave himself up for the happiness of others. His entire life was an illustration of the famous description of love in 1 Corinthians 13. If you read about Jesus in the Gospels, you don't get the impression he was a repressed, frustrated person who was so bound up by rules that his life was lacking. Rather, you see a fulfilled person, a man with a sense of purpose in life, a man whose joy was giving to others. This is what makes it all the more tragic that Jesus ended up being executed. The Bible makes it clear that good people often do suffer persecution. We know this instinctively, and we see it everyday in the news. Yet deep down, we also know that being good is good itself. It is its own reward.

A moment ago we were dealing with one moral problem—pornography—and how we could apply the Bible to it. Strictly speaking, the Bible says nothing about pornography. It does have a lot to say about keeping our minds out of the gutter. Nowhere in the Bible will you find a rule saying, "You shall not watch X-rated videos." Rather, you would find an image of life that allows no place for something like pornography. The Bible's answer is not, "Don't watch that video." The Bible's answer is, "Haven't you got something better to do with your life?"

You may face a choice in life where you will want to turn to the Bible and ask, "What can it tell me about the best decision to make in this situation?" This is a valid way to use the Bible. But equally valid is studying the Bible on a regular basis so that you'll already have an idea of the kind of life God wants you to lead.

Put another way, the best way you can use the Bible in moral decision making is to know the Bible well. That can't happen overnight, and it doesn't need to.

God doesn't want followers who are nothing more than a bunch of robots who slavishly follow rules because we have to. God knows that things done strictly out of duty are not very fulfilling—either to him or to us. Doing things because we want to—or, even better, *because we love someone*—is fulfilling. God's rule—a very good one—tells us not to murder an enemy. But love can go beyond that, telling us to aid a wounded enemy. God is pleased when we don't murder. He is even more pleased when we go beyond the rules and act lovingly.

If you think back to your early childhood, you might recall times when you were eager to please a parent. When a parent asked, "Sandy, would you like to help me set the table?" you replied, "Yes!" Why? Because small children seem to have a natural desire to please their parents in any way they can. As the years pass, this desire seems to go away. How many teenagers have that same wide-eyed eagerness? If you read the Bible (especially the New Testament) closely, you can see some of that childhood innocence recaptured. The first Christians felt it—that amazing desire to please God. That desire, more than any set of rules, was what guided their behavior. People can still feel that today, but not so long as they have a negative attitude toward rules or to the One who is the final authority.

4. Learn to pray.

You'll find a separate chapter on prayer in this book (pages 163-77). We won't cover all that material here, except to say that it is perfectly right for you to pray to God for guidance in life. Again and again the Bible shows people pouring out their hearts to God. Even if our prayers aren't clever or eloquent, God listens. He is pleased to have people come to him for guidance.

One question people ask is, How will I know God has answered my prayer? In a few places the Bible tells of God speaking in an audible voice. Some people today claim this has happened to them. But more often people hear an "inner voice"—God speaking through their mind. Can they be 100 percent sure this is God? What if they're just hearing their own wishful thinking?

One way to know is to ask, Does this message from God contradict what the Bible teaches about God? If it does, it can't be right. God, as the Bible shows, is consistent. He doesn't contradict himself. If a man prays, "God, should I leave my wife and marry my secretary?" he might think he hears God saying to him, "Yes, your present marriage isn't so great, and you owe yourself some pleasure now." The man's own mind might be telling him that, but God wouldn't. What if a woman prayed, "Lord, I'm facing a career choice. This new job has more pay and prestige, but I'd do a lot of traveling and spend a lot more time away from my family. Should I take the job?" The woman's inner voice might say, "Sure, everyone is entitled to a fulfilling career." But if she knows the Bible's view of self-giving love, she would know that God would not urge someone to take a job that would cause that person to neglect his or her family.

Praying and expecting an answer from God is not a shortcut to knowing his clear will revealed in the Bible. People have believed for centuries that the Bible reveals God to us. We need to know that revelation well. We also need to pray so that the God of the

Bible can also communicate with us personally. But we need to realize that, in the area of decision making, the Bible is "home base." It is the foundation for decision making, and we ought to consult it before deciding whether we ought to pray about a particular decision.

> "In all my perplexities and distresses the Bible has never failed to give me light and strength."
>
> ROBERT E. LEE,
> CONFEDERATE GENERAL
> (1807–1870)

Let's consider an analogy: You make a rule that your children can't have sweets before meals. It's a sensible rule, and your children hear the rule often enough that they know it well. So if one of your children comes to you just before dinner and asks, "Can I have some ice cream now?" how do you respond? You'd probably say, "Haven't I already said you can't do that?"

But what about major decisions that aren't covered in the Bible? For example, a childless couple has learned that they can adopt three siblings—all three, or none. The couple faces a choice: 1) Adopt all three (which means going from a two-person household to a five-person household overnight); 2) wait, and hope that later on they will have an opportunity to adopt just one child; or 3) risk the possibility that they might never again have the chance to adopt. The Bible gives no direct guidance in a matter like this. Wanting children is a moral thing. So is living without children. So is adopting—whether one child or three. There are no "wrong" choices, strictly speaking. But the couple prays, hoping that God will guide them toward the *best* decision. It is perfectly right to pray in this way. Later on, the couple might believe that God gave them an answer—maybe through an audible voice, or through an inward one. Or they might believe that they received no answer at all. The Bible does not promise us that God will give a clear answer in all situations. Sometimes he does, and sometimes he doesn't. In this case, what matters is that the couple studied the matter carefully, made sure that none of their choices went against God's clear commands, then made a choice. We can do no more than that, except to ask God to give us courage to live with the consequences of what we choose.

5. Ask advice of people you respect.

Moral decision making is more than just "me, the Bible, and God." Wisdom comes through other people, including parents. Of course, we wouldn't want advice from people who aren't particularly wise or moral. If certain individuals haven't made a success (morally speaking) of their lives, it's not a good idea to follow their advice. But you probably know at least a few people who have managed to live a moral (and happy) life. What is their secret? Have they struggled with some of the same moral dilemmas that you have? If so, give them a listen.

In times past, people often turned to their pastor for advice. If you don't attend a church, you probably don't know any pastors, and I wouldn't recommend you just choose one at random. If you do attend a church and your pastor is someone whose opinion you respect, consider him as one possible source of guidance. But don't assume that all pastors have a high opinion of the Bible. Many do, but some don't. Some pastors are more interested in advancing some social agenda rather than in helping people find personal guidance through the Bible.

Don't assume that education necessarily has a positive effect on a person's morals. I knew professors in undergraduate and graduate school who were shining lights of morality and good sense. But I also knew some who were quite the opposite. If you're seeking some wisdom to live by, don't let a college degree (or lack of it) influence who you listen to. Educated people tend to assume that, having "gotten their smarts" after years of education, they know how to lead a moral life. Some of them are more than happy to pass on their wisdom (or lack of it) to others. And some of them are so good with words and so good at appearing knowledgeable that they can always get someone to listen to them. Yet there are intellectuals who have no morals—just as there are cleaning women and garbage collectors who do have morals. Remember that the Nazi torturers who designed and ran the concentration camps in Germany during World War II were intelligent, well educated, and cultured. And they were evil.

6. Don't agonize when you don't have to.

God likes people who pay attention to their consciences. In a world where so many people seem to throw morality to the wind, God is pleased with those who take morals seriously. A man who agonizes over his extramarital fling is more pleasing to God than a man who has a fling and feels no guilt at all. (Of course, the man who resists the temptation to have the fling is even more pleasing to God.) Morals do matter. We don't need to feel ashamed that we are aiming for a better life than many people aim for.

> "It is impossible mentally or socially to enslave a Bible-reading people."
>
> HORACE GREELEY,
> AMERICAN JOURNALIST
> (1811–1872; FAMOUS FOR COINING THE PHRASE,
> "GO WEST, YOUNG MAN.")

But we also don't need to agonize over things that aren't important. I have known some very moral people who, alas, agonized over everything. I knew a pastor who prayed every Sunday about which color suit he should wear into the pulpit. Did it matter? He believed it did because he believed that God cares about every aspect of our lives. Well, he was right about that specific point. He was right to believe God wants us to honor him in everything we do. But when you read the Bible, you'll see that God is deeply concerned with our *hearts*—that is, who we are on the inside. That's what deserves our attention. We should not wear ourselves out worrying about every tiny aspect of our lives. God made us for something better than anxiety and worry.

The more familiar you are with the Bible, the more you notice that *respect* is a key theme. You won't find the word itself very often, but the idea is present, loud and clear. The usual synonym for it is *love,* which, unfortunately, is a word we associate with being "in love." But in the Bible, *love* can mean "respect" and "concern." We are supposed to respect God by worshipping only him. We are supposed to respect authority figures (such as our parents). We are supposed to respect other people's property (by not stealing or swindling) and life (by not killing or injuring). We are supposed to respect the truth (by not lying to benefit ourselves or harm other people). The Bible indicates that we can enjoy life immensely and have a fine time *so long as we give the proper respect to others.* Our wants and needs and rights are not problems unless they infringe on what we owe others. When it comes to making a decision, we need to ask, Am I showing the respect I owe to God and to other people? If the answer is a clear no, then we need to give the situation some more thought.

Asking this question can also save you a lot of grief over unimportant things. Shall I wear my blue suit or my gray? Shall I have coffee or tea with breakfast? Shall I take the kids to Disney World or camping? If neither choice shows disrespect for God or others, don't agonize over it.

7. Learn to enjoy your freedom.

Should you cheat on your income tax? No. Should you have a glass of wine with dinner? Well, the Bible does not answer that. It does mention people (including Jesus) drinking wine. It also shows the abuse that drunkenness leads to. For this reason, some people choose not to drink at all. But they can't, strictly speaking, claim that the Bible tells them to avoid wine. It doesn't. It is their own choice, but not one they can impose on other people. We should respect someone who can enjoy a glass of wine with dinner. We should respect someone who chooses not to. Neither person is doing anything immoral.

But it *is* immoral to create rules that we don't need. You'll find this mentioned in the letters of Paul. The early Christians believed that Jesus was their Savior, the one who blotted out their sins and made them right with God. Because they had a Savior, they were not bound by all the Jewish laws concerning kosher food, animal sacrifice, working on the sabbath, etc. But Paul discovered something that is still true today: People like to create rules for themselves. We hate rules, yet we like them, too. Why? Because if we create rules of our own (rules we can obey, obviously), we can feel good about measuring up to them. We use rules to feel better about ourselves. But it's not the mere act of following rules that makes us better.

People were the same way in the New Testament period. Paul gave a resounding *no!* to this. Again and again he talked about *freedom*—not freedom from all moral laws, but freedom from silly regulations that have no importance to God. Paul's letter to the Galatians mentioned this. Paul told the Christians of Galatia that they had been "bewitched" by the "rule-makers" who were trying to impose man-made restrictions on them (Galatians 3:1-3).

In 1 Corinthians, Paul dealt with the same problem: Some people were claiming to be more spiritual because they followed certain rules. Paul's advice? Respect each other's differences over nonessentials. There are too many things that really matter for us to waste time bickering over things that don't matter. And, we aren't to sneer at people who choose to avoid things that we ourselves can enjoy. Nor are they to sneer at us. It is possible for us to have morals and, at the same time, to say, regarding some minor matters, "Do your own thing." The more we study the Bible, the more we will understand what those minor matters are.

A word about the "new morality": more accurately, this is the new "social consciousness," which is particularly manifest in the form of environmental concern. The Bible shows a deep appreciation for the natural world, but not to the point of worshipping it. In this day in which the "Love Your Mother" (earth, that is) slogan is on bumper stickers everywhere, it is easy to be sucked in by the new morality of earth worship. How can we be a concerned person? By recycling, not using our car unless we have to, giving money to environmentalist causes, etc. If you do any of those things, fine. But don't get too carried away by your "enlightened consciousness." The Bible doesn't present environmental concern as one of the marks of a moral person.

8. Remember God.

The first words of the Bible are, "In the beginning God...." God is the main character from beginning to end. The Bible is saturated with God, and you can't read more than a few pages without realizing that the Bible authors believed firmly that God was watching them. This is a pleasant thought (since God watches over us with love), but also an intimidating one (God is aware of everything we do). Like the carnival fortune-teller, God "sees all, knows all"—except that, unlike the fortune-teller, God really does know all. In the words of Jesus, "There is nothing concealed that will not be disclosed, or hidden that will not be made known. What you have said in the dark will be heard in the daylight, and what you have whispered in the ear in the inner rooms will be proclaimed from the roofs" (Luke 12:2-3). This belief is assumed on every page of the Bible. No matter where we are or what we do, God sees all.

It is easy to forget this in our contemporary situation. In earlier days, when people lived in smaller towns and could observe each other more closely, it was natural to believe that someone was watching—since someone probably was. Today, with sprawling cities and people moving frequently, we can be surrounded by strangers who don't care whether we're moral people or not. (In fact, we're likely to live among people who would be happy to encourage us in immoral behavior.) Given this situation, it is easy to forget that someone—or Someone—is watching over us. We can deceive ourselves into thinking that our actions don't matter, for no one will confront us.

Reading the Bible often is a healthful corrective to this. The more you read the Bible and the more seriously you take it, the more likely you are to ask yourself, What does God think about what I'm doing right now? Sometimes we may rightly conclude that God wouldn't mind at all. Does God mind if you walk your dog in the park? No. Does God mind if you pay for your girlfriend to have an abortion? Yes. Who knows how many wrongs would cease if people asked themselves, Does God really want me to do this? It's such a simple, childlike question, but one that is very basic to morals and decision making. It is the idea behind the part of the Lord's prayer that says to God, "Your will be done" (Matthew 6:10).

9. Remember God's forgiveness.

God is not a cosmic killjoy. He is, according to the Bible, a Father, so his rules for us are for our benefit. He is not an *indulgent* Father, which means he punishes (or, looked at another way, he sometimes lets us suffer the consequences of our failings). But above all, he is a forgiving Father, a "God of new beginnings" who is always willing to receive us when we want to change. The story of the prodigal son and the forgiving father in Luke 15 is a touching illustration of just how merciful God is.

> "We are not at liberty to pick and choose out of its contents, but must receive it all as we find it."
>
> JOHN HENRY NEWMAN,
> ENGLISH CATHOLIC LEADER
> (1801–1890)

On the practical level, this means two things: One, because God is a loving Father, we ought to live to please him. This, and not a fear of breaking the rules, is to be the motivating force in our lives. God loves us. When we love him, morality is easier because we *want* to do the right thing.

Two, because God forgives, we are free to fail. You probably remember your parents or teachers using that tired old analogy about learning to ride a horse: "When you fall off that horse, get right back on again till you get it right." That's exactly how we ought to approach our own morals. We fail, inevitably. It's tempting to get discouraged. After all, we've made so many mistakes that we're sure we're going to make others. But according to the Bible, God is pleased when we desire to do what is right.

10. Emphasize the small things.

For most people in most situations, living a moral life involves dozens of little daily decisions, not big ones. In our daily lives we seldom face the "biggies," such as murder, adultery, and theft. We make little choices, such as gossiping over a fellow worker, buying a certain type of magazine, watching a particular TV show, showing our crankiness to the other drivers on the freeway, joining gleefully in a gripe session. In most of these situations we are not facing great moral dilemmas, but rather little choices about how we spend our time and mental energy.

More often than not, these small moral choices involve that vicious organ of the body called the tongue. The Bible has a great deal to say about our words and the harm they can do. The authors of the Bible understood that basic human need of "information compulsion"—that desire to pass on information we know to someone else. If this is merely a matter of telling your neighbor how well your new car runs, fine. But sometimes information compulsion can do a great deal of harm to others. James 3 is the Bible's chapter par excellence on the harm we can do with our speech.

Key Ethical Passages in the Bible

The passages listed here are not the only parts of the Bible that relate to morals and decision making. They are the key passages, and they contain the essence of what the Bible teaches about our moral life.

The Ten Commandments
Exodus 20:1-17
Deuteronomy 5:1-20

Jesus' Sermon on the Mount
Matthew 5–7

Love
Matthew 22:34-40
John 14:15-21; 15:9-17
1 Corinthians 13
Galatians 5:22-23
Ephesians 5:1-2
Colossians 3:12-14
1 John 2:5-17; 3:7-24

Practical advice on everyday living
The book of Proverbs

Priorities in life
Matthew 4:1-11; 6:25-34
Mark 8:34-38
Luke 10:25-37; 12:13-34
Romans 12:1-2
1 Corinthians 1:20-31
1 Timothy 6:3-10
1 John 2:15-17

Injustice and oppression
Amos 5–6
Micah 6:8

Husbands and wives
Proverbs 5:20; 12:4; 18:22; 31:10-31
Matthew 5:27-32
1 Corinthians 7
Ephesians 5:22-43
Colossians 3:18-19
Hebrews 13:4
1 Peter 3:1-7

Parents and children
Proverbs 13:1; 17:6; 19:26; 22:6; 23:13
Ephesians 6:1-4
Colossians 3:20-21

Sexual morality
Matthew 5:27-32
Matthew 15:19
Romans 1:18-32

Romans 13:12-14
1 Corinthians 5–7
Galatians 5:19-26
Colossians 3:1-17
1 Thessalonians 4:3-8
Revelation 21:8

Gossip, criticism, judgment
Matthew 7:1-2; 15:19-20
Romans 1:28-31

IS "BE KIND TO ANIMALS" IN THE BIBLE?

We know that the Bible tells us to love God and our fellow human beings. Does it tell us to love animals?

Yes and no. In an agricultural society (which we find in both the Old and New Testaments), people aren't usually sentimental about animals. Most animals are viewed as means for food or farming or transportation. And the Bible never mentions pets. (Dogs, by the way, were not pets in Bible times. They were half-wild scavengers, and people despised them.)

But mercy is highly valued in the Bible. We are even encouraged to extend it to birds and animals: "If you come across a bird's nest beside the road, either in a tree or on the ground, and the mother is sitting on the young or on the eggs, do not take the mother with the young. You may take the young, but be sure to let the mother go, so that it may go well with you and you may have a long life" (Deuteronomy 22:6-7).

Note that this isn't just good advice. It is a direct command from the Lord. As Jesus said, God does have concern for his creation, even for birds: "Are not two sparrows sold for a penny? Yet not one of them will fall to the ground apart from the will of your Father" (Matthew 10:29).

Ephesians 4:31
Colossians 3:8
James 3:1-12; 4:11-12

Freedom from legalism
1 Corinthians 8:1–11:1
Galatians
Colossians 2:6-23

Dealing with temptation
Proverbs 2:10-12
1 Corinthians 10:12-13
Hebrews 2:14-18
James 1:2-15

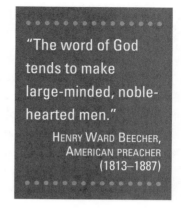

"The word of God tends to make large-minded, noble-hearted men."

HENRY WARD BEECHER,
AMERICAN PREACHER
(1813–1887)

If you have a reference book called a *topical Bible,* you can look up topics alphabetically and find all the Bible passages that relate to that topic. You could look up, for example, *marriage, career, infidelity, friendship, temptation, children,* and so on. For more information on topical Bibles, see page 237.

Also, on pages 114-130 you'll find information on different ways to approach Bible study. You'll note that in every one of the different approaches, *application* is important—that is, in any Bible study you should ask yourself, *How does this apply to my life?* Doing this on a regular basis is the best means for getting the Bible into you so that, when you need to make important decisions, you'll already have the Bible in your mind and heart.

SOME THINGS NEVER CHANGE...

The ancient world was a violent place. There were no assault rifles or nuclear weapons, but there were plenty of swords, knives, spears, and such. The book of Psalms contains songs directed against the cruel enemies of Israel. Naturally, these poems contain references to weapons of war and destruction.

But in fact the authors of the psalms spent a lot more time talking about a *really* dangerous weapon:

> You destroy those who tell lies; bloodthirsty and deceitful men the LORD abhors (5:6).

> Not a word from their mouth can be trusted; their heart is filled with destruction. Their throat is an open grave; with their tongue they speak deceit (5:9).

> His mouth is full of curses and lies and threats; trouble and evil are under his tongue (10:7).

> Everyone lies to his neighbor; their flattering lips speak with deception (12:2).

> You use your mouth for evil and harness your tongue to deceit (50:19).

> Your tongue plots destruction; it is like a sharpened razor, you who practice deceit (52:2).

> They sharpen their tongues like swords and aim their words like deadly arrows (64:3).

> All day long my enemies taunt me; those who rail against me use my name as a curse (102:8).

> They make their tongues as sharp as a serpent's; the poison of vipers is on their lips (140:3).

These are the tip of the iceberg. There are many more similar verses from the psalms. The book of Psalms has been called many things. It could be called "The Book of God's Contempt for Cruel Speech." The psalmists were apparently well acquainted with the weapon that did more harm than all the swords of the Babylonians and Assyrians.

The Psalms' view of the lethal power of the tongue reflects the whole Bible's view. Both the Old and New Testaments make it clear that God has a low view of people who use their tongues to do harm.

7

Conversing with God:

LEARNING TO PRAY WITH THE BIBLE

To an unbeliever, prayer may seem like talking to oneself. But for the Christian, prayer is conversing with God, addressing the Almighty. This conversation can take place anywhere, anytime. There are no "sacred places" for prayer, since God is everywhere. In the Bible, we find people praying in the temple, outdoors, indoors, standing, and lying down. Prayer can take the form of praise, adoration, thanksgiving, requests (even questioning), tears, anguish, anger. In the Bible's view, the worst kind of prayer is no prayer. Not praying means, in practice, atheism. If we don't pray, we're acting as if God, the Ruler of the universe and of us, didn't exist. Not praying at all is like entering a house and ignoring the person who owns it.

The Bible is full of prayer. The longest book of the Bible, Psalms, consists of 150 poems that are mainly addressed to God. They run the gamut of human emotions. There is probably nothing you've ever thought about saying to God that is not somewhere expressed in Psalms, which is the "prayer book" of God's people. The first Christians inherited the book from the Jews and accepted it as their own. Psalms is the most-quoted Old Testament book in the New Testament. Throughout the world, Christians every Sunday read, chant, or sing a psalm during their worship. One long prayer, Psalm 119, is the longest prayer in the Bible, and also the longest chapter.

We can find prayers scattered elsewhere in the Bible. Smack in the middle of the historical books are prayers of thanksgiving, requests, even anguish and despair. All the key Bible characters prayed. Some, like the reluctant prophet Jonah, found themselves praying in odd places (the belly of a "great fish" in Jonah's case). The prophet Elijah, on the lam from wicked Queen Jezebel, prayed that God would take his life (an anguished request that, happily, God did not grant). Jesus taught the importance of prayer and gave the famous Lord's Prayer as a role model.

Churches that are *liturgical*—Catholic, Episcopalian, Orthodox, and some others—use books of prayer. These printed prayers often use language straight from the Bible, and they cover a wide range of subjects—prayers for healing, prayers for rain, prayers of thanksgiving, etc. These "fixed" prayers serve a purpose: People can look up an appropriate prayer for almost any occasion. But there's a problem with this practice: A person who depends on these may never learn to pray on his own. And it is clear in the Bible that each individual can and must address himself to God. Eloquence and cleverness are not important. What counts is honestly expressing to God our feelings and thoughts, both good and bad.

As for how to pray, the Bible can help us with this.

Prayer 101: The Lord's Prayer

Consider the great model for prayers, the Lord's Prayer. The version found in Matthew's Gospel reads this way: "Our Father in heaven, hallowed be your name, your kingdom come, your will be done on earth as it is in heaven. Give us today our daily bread. Forgive us our debts, as we also have forgiven our debtors. And lead us not into temptation, but deliver us from the evil one" (Matthew 6:9-13).

Jesus prefaced this prayer by saying, "Pray in this way," not "This is the exact prayer you should repeat every day." In other words, the prayer was a model—a pattern by which we can flesh out a prayer with our own individual words.

What does the model consist of? It acknowledges God as "our Father." God is not some distant, cold Being. He is a Father with a close relationship to those who are his children. He is in heaven—meaning not the sky or outer space, but "above us," spiritually speaking. (If he is not, why bother praying to him at all?) The word "Father" conveys the idea of authority; in the Bible's view, a child is duty-bound to obey his father. So calling God "Father" carries the message, "I'm here in an attitude of respect, willing to obey you."

"Hallowed be your name" is simple enough: God is holy and sacred. Calling on him by name involves reverence on our part. Even though we have just called him "Father," this One whom we pray to is to be approached with respect and honor. In a day when so many people don't take the Bible or religion seriously, it is easy to forget that in ages past people had an awe of God. Even if they saw him as loving and kind, they remembered that he was the Almighty—a powerful Father, not a creampuff daddy. Jesus was telling his disciples that when they approached their Father, they needed to recall that he was a power to be reckoned with. All the prayers in the Bible assume this—even prayers that complain to God.

"Your kingdom come" means "I desire your rule (including your rule over myself)." Notice that before the prayer mentions any of our own needs, it first expresses a wish for God's rule. (In Jesus' day, it was assumed that a ruler's will could—and should—override anyone else's.) "Your will be done" acknowledges that we desire God to accomplish what he will. It is a way of saying that our desires are aligned with his, or that we want them to be. It also means that we accept that God's desire has priority over our own. That seems appropriate, if he truly is the Almighty and all-knowing One. "Your will be done" isn't just a general way of saying "I hope the universe is going the way you like it." More specifically, it is saying, "May your will be done *in me.*" In many prayers in the Bible, the person who is praying is expressing a willingness to hold up his own life for God's inspection and use.

"Give us today our daily bread" means we ask for what we need, not what we *want* (which might not be good for us). The Bible never says we can pray for a luxury car and get one. But Jesus made it clear in many of his sayings that God the Father would supply his children with what they really need in this life. This part of the prayer makes it clear that praying for riches, fame, worldly power, etc., is wrong. We may *want* those things, but we have no business asking God to provide us with them. (At the same time, it is perfectly right to thank God for letting us have good things to enjoy—even a luxury car, if we happen to own one.)

"Give us today our daily bread" reminds us of something else: We are needy creatures. Nothing in the Bible indicates that we *deserve* anything. So the prayer says, "Give us"—a polite request, not a demand. God does not owe us anything, but the Bible makes it clear that he does supply us with what we need anyway.

"Forgive us our debts" isn't referring to financial debts. It refers to wrongs we've done. (The version of the Lord's Prayer in Luke's Gospel uses the word "sins" instead of "debts," which makes the meaning more obvious.) The prayer is saying, "Forgive our wrongs to others, and we forgive people's wrongs to us." This is a key idea in the New Testament: We are to forgive others because God forgives us. Be kind, because Someone has been kind to you. God is a God of mercy. To be near him, we have to show mercy, also. (If we believe this, we also have to believe that we should never pray for something bad to happen to someone else, not even someone who has hurt us deeply.)

"Lead us not into temptation" confuses some people. Would a loving Father really lead his children into a bad situation? Today's English Version is a little clearer: "Do not lead us to hard testing." The prayer continues "but deliver us from the evil one." This refers to Satan, of course. Satan, the evil one, is also the "tester"—the one who "shows us what we're made of."

"For yours is the kingdom and the power and the glory forever. Amen." (In the NIV, this closing line usually appears in a footnote.) The prayer ends up where it started by acknowledging God as the Almighty One. So the model prayer is a kind of sandwich: Our needs and requests to God are sandwiched between our praises of God, which testify to his authority. The model indicates that the right kind of prayer is polite—that is, we don't come storming in to God like a spoiled brat, making ridiculous requests. First we acknowledge who we're dealing with, and only then do we ask for our needs to be met. (A comparison: If you had a problem you wanted to discuss with your boss, you wouldn't just barge in to his office. First you would ask, politely, if you could discuss the matter. And upon finishing the discussion, you would politely leave the office, not go stomping out—not if you're smart, anyway, since you know your boss is in control of the situation. And God deserves more consideration than a human boss.)

Not every prayer in the Bible follows the Lord's Prayer model. But in a very general sense, many do. Throughout the Bible we see people approaching God as the Almighty King. In their prayer, they bow (mentally, if not physically) before making a request. Perhaps our contemporary sloppiness about manners keeps us from appreciating this. And perhaps the flippancy so often expressed in interpersonal relationships today keeps us from grasping the importance of showing respect to an authority figure. The God of the Bible is not just "dear old Dad," he's the "monarch of all things."

Praying in Jesus' Name

You may have heard people end a prayer with the words, "We ask these things in Jesus' name. Amen." Like the use of "amen," the use of "ask these things in Jesus' name" is often a habit, one so ingrained that most people have no idea what it means. It is much like asking someone, "How are you?" when we aren't really concerned about their answer. But this habit of praying in Jesus' name is based on a promise Jesus made: "My Father will give you whatever you ask in my name" (John 16:23). This is just one of several "my name" promises Jesus made:

> Where two or three come together in my name, there am I with them (Matthew 18:20).

> I will do whatever you ask in my name, so that the Son may bring glory to the Father. You may ask me for anything in my name, and I will do it (John 14:13-14).

People are inclined to misinterpret this. After all, it sounds like a blank check—just ask God for something, and you get it. But this is a case where you have to measure a part of the Bible against the whole. Does the Bible *as a whole* tell us God will give us anything we want? No, indeed. So just what was Jesus promising, then?

"In my name" doesn't just mean "using my name." It means "on my behalf." If you work for the mayor and rent a car "in his name" (on his behalf, that is), you better be using it for his official business and not for your own personal pleasure. When Jesus said, "My Father will give you whatever you ask in my name," he was talking about things asked on his behalf. If we are asking "in his name"—on his behalf—we aren't asking for a Caribbean cruise or a BMW. We know full well those aren't things he would ask for himself. But we could "in his name" ask for strength to get through a difficult situation, or we could ask for more energy to do things we need to do, or for wisdom in managing our family. A helpful test for us using "in his name" is this: If Jesus were standing next to you, would you be ashamed to make this request? If so, then it isn't something you would request on his behalf.

So, when you or someone else ends a prayer with "in Jesus' name," realize that the words are more than just a formula, more than just "magic words" tacked onto the end of a prayer. In fact, nowhere does the Bible say you are under compulsion to ever say those words. You are asked to pray *on Jesus' behalf.* Paul caught the idea pretty well when he told the Corinthian Christians, "We are therefore Christ's ambassadors" (2 Corinthians 5:20).

The word *hallelujah* (or *alleluia*) is often used in Christian worship and prayer. The only New Testament book to use it is the book of Revelation (19:1,3-4,6). But the Hebrew word *hallelujah* occurs many times in the book of Psalms. It is translated as "praise the Lord."

But Can We Be Just a Little Selfish?

Is it selfish to ask for healing of a disease? Selfish to ask for an end to financial trouble? For a less stressful job? Are these prayers as selfish as praying for a new Jaguar?

No, they aren't. The people of the Bible poured out their requests and their anguish to God in a big way. The classic example is Psalm 22, which begins, "My God, my God, why have you forsaken me? Why are you so far from saving me, so far from the words of my groaning?" Whatever was afflicting this poor soul, he didn't hesitate to put it into words. Interestingly, while Jesus was hanging from the cross, he uttered these words. We should feel good that he did. It meant he was truly human, even if he was the Son of God. It meant that we, in the midst of pain, are not wrong to ask, "Why, God?"

Psalm 22, of course, is an extreme example. In most cases, the people of the Bible who prayed to God were in less anguish than the author of Psalm 22. Another example of one who had some sort of trouble is the apostle Paul: "There was given me a thorn in my flesh, a messenger of Satan, to torment me. Three times I pleaded with the Lord to take it away from me. But he said to me, 'My grace is sufficient for you, for my power is made perfect in weakness'" (2 Corinthians 12:7-9). We don't know what Paul's "thorn" was—something serious, obviously. He prayed that it be removed, and there is no indication it was improper for him to ask this. God's answer was not, in this case, to grant the request. But elsewhere in the Bible, many people do get what they pray for. Jesus and the apostles healed many people who came to them for help. There is never a hint that it is selfish to want to be healthy and whole. So praying for mental and physical health—our own, or anyone else's—is fine.

What about death? Most people won't pray that a dead person be brought back to life (even though this occurred a few times in the Bible). But many people do pray that they, or someone whom they love, be spared from death. This happened many times in the Bible. In fact, Jesus himself asked to be spared. But he ended his prayer by saying to God, "Yet not what I will, but what you will"

(Mark 14:36). (Remember the part of the Lord's Prayer that asks, "Your will be done.") Sometimes people are spared, sometimes not. But to pray for it is not wrong.

Praying on Other People's Behalf

It is easy to pray for our friends. But what about our enemies? The Bible says we should pray for them. Hanging from a cross, Jesus said, "Father, forgive them" (Luke 23:34)—a hard thing for him to say, no doubt. We are supposed to do the same. Did anyone say this was easy? It isn't. Nothing in the Bible goes against our grain like asking God's favor on people we dislike. But the Bible never tells us we have to like these people or enjoy their company—that may not even be possible. It tells us to show them mercy, even in our prayers. Someone whom we secretly dislike is also someone we should secretly pray for.

Jesus prayed for other people, not just himself. The New Testament tells us to do the same. It even tells us to pray for government officials. First Timothy 2:1-4 says,

> I urge, then, first of all, that requests, prayers, intercession and thanksgiving be made for everyone—for kings and all those in authority, that we may live peaceful and quiet lives in all godliness and holiness. This is good, and pleases God our Savior, who wants all men to be saved and to come to a knowledge of the truth.

Note that the verses don't tell us we have to admire or like officials. But we are told to pray for them—and rightly so, since their actions affect so many people. It makes sense. The same applies to others who are in positions of authority—employers, for example.

An important point: Praying for someone else, even a longtime enemy, has a very positive effect on us. It can help take our mind off our petty grievances. The Bible is anti-selfishness on every page. It presents a God who is pleased when we take a genuine interest in other people's welfare.

GRACE BEFORE DINNER?

The old practice of saying a prayer before a meal is dying out. But the practice isn't completely dead. For many people, the only memory they have of praying is the memory of someone saying grace or a blessing before a meal.

Is this practice in the Bible? Indeed it is. The person most noted for practicing it was Jesus himself. Several places in the Gospels mention him giving thanks before eating. The Gospels even mention that he "looked up to heaven" when he gave thanks (Mark 6:41). But Jesus' behavior wasn't unusual. He was doing what devout Jews of his era did. When he said, in the Lord's Prayer, "give us today our daily bread," he had more than just bread in mind. But he, and any faithful Jew at that time, would have made sure that he did at least thank God for his "daily bread."

Thank You Very Kindly

The Bible doesn't offer support for the self-centered "gimme, gimme" prayer. It does tell us to give thanks for the things we receive. Of all the prayers in the Bible, there are more prayers of thanksgiving than prayers with requests.

Thanksgiving, or gratitude, isn't quite the same as praise. Praising God is like praising an admirable person we like: "Wow, you're wonderful—I just have to tell you!" Thanksgiving is the expression of gratitude for something done for us. Paul, in his letters, gives thanks to God again and again. His classic statement on gratitude is in 1 Thessalonians: "Give thanks in all circumstances, for this is God's will for you in Christ Jesus" (5:18). Thanks doesn't come naturally to most people. It's easy to give thanks for something good, but to "give thanks in all circumstances"? According to the Bible, yes, we should be thankful in good times or bad. It is easy to ridicule the eternal optimist who says, "Well, I didn't get that promotion I wanted, but at least I'll have more time to spend with my family." But in the Bible's view, this is a healthy attitude—finding the good in situations that seem bad.

Baring Our Souls

The people of the Bible had more of a sin-consciousness than do most people today. That's probably because they had a high awareness that God is very moral and offended by human sin. Most people believed that God had told them how to live morally, and if they failed, they should confess their failings to him. But one of the great joys in life is that God forgives—again and again, in fact. But this divine forgiveness hinges on one thing: the willingness to admit we did wrong. If there is no repentance, then there is no forgiveness. If there is no confession, then there is no fellowship with God. You never see a hint in the Bible that we can evade responsibility for what we've done. "Well, the reason I left my wife was...." "I had a very unhappy childhood, so...." "I've been abused, so it's no wonder I...." These excuses may get people off the hook in the human court, but not (according to the Bible) in God's court.

Psalm 32 shows how one anguished soul found release: "I acknowledged my sin to you and did not cover up my iniquity. I said, 'I will confess my transgressions to the Lord'—and you forgave the guilt of my sin."

The New Testament presents the same idea: "If we confess our sins, he is faithful and just and will forgive us our sins and purify us from all unrighteousness" (1 John 1:9).

As the Bible sees it, we owe this to God. We follow the same idea in human relations. If we injure or offend someone, we make an apology and ask for forgiveness. Then, to prove we're sincere, we do better. The person should, if he is fair-minded and merciful, forgive us. This doesn't always happen. But according to the Bible, it always happens with God. He never fails to forgive the person who is truly sorry.

THE STRANGEST PLACE TO PRAY

"They took Jonah and threw him overboard.... But the LORD provided a great fish to swallow Jonah, and Jonah was inside the fish three days and three nights. From inside the fish Jonah prayed to the LORD his God" (Jonah 1:15,17–2:1).

Can we get people today to accept the Bible's view of the seriousness of sin? That's a tough one. Maybe the word *sin* itself seems outdated. But ten minutes of channel-surfing on the television will convince you that people *do* feel a sense of something being wrong—"I know I need help," or "I know I need to grow in the area of...." In other words, people are very aware that they've "missed the mark" in some part of their lives. And this is exactly what sin means in the Bible—missing the mark, or failing to be what we should be. The Bible offers an "out" for us: Instead of flitting like a butterfly from one self-help plan or guru to another, we begin (and end) with God, saying, "I'm not all I should be. I've failed in many ways. I'm eager to start fresh, to make a new beginning." The Bible presents us with a God who says, "I can accept that. Now, let's get to work on you...."

Key Bible Passages Concerning Prayer

If you want to learn to pray, the Bible offers two kinds of passages: those concerned with prayer, and model prayers themselves.

Passages on Prayer
> Proverbs 15:8; 28:9
> Isaiah 1:15
> Matthew 5:44
> Matthew 6:9-13
> Mark 11:25-26
> Luke 11:5-8
> Luke 18:1-14

John 16:23-24
Romans 8:15-16,26,34
Romans 12:12
Ephesians 3:16-17
Ephesians 6:18
Philippians 4:6
Colossians 4:2
2 Thessalonians 3:1-2
1 Timothy 2:1,8
Hebrews 5:7
1 Peter 3:12
James 5:13-18
1 John 1:9

Model Prayers

Praying for others
Genesis 18:16-33
Genesis 25:21
Exodus 32:11-13
1 Samuel 12:23
1 Kings 8:22-53
2 Kings 19:14-19
John 17

For help
Genesis 32:9-11
1 Samuel 1:9-18
Psalm 3–7; 12–13; 17; 28; 35; 69; 88; 130
Matthew 26:39-44

For guidance
Psalm 25

For justice
Psalm 10; 54

Praising God
1 Samuel 2:1-10
1 Chronicles 29:10-13
Psalm 8; 9; 16; 18; 19; 24; 27; 100; 103
Luke 1:46-55,68-79

Thanking God
Psalm 30; 40; 65; 92; 116
Jonah 2

Confessing sins
Psalm 32; 51

Confidence in God
Psalm 139

Pain and anguish
1 Kings 19:1-9
Psalm 22; 38; 39; 41; 109; 130
Isaiah 38
Jonah 2:2-9

Longing for God
Psalm 63; 84

What Does *Amen* Mean?

Amen is a permanent part of our language, even among people who have no religious leanings at all. An older generation remembers when a pastor's sermon would be punctuated with an approving "Amen!" from individuals in the church. Today, *amen* is more likely to be used in a joking way.

It isn't a joking matter in the Bible. *Amen* is a Hebrew word used often in the Old Testament. Loosely translated (although no one ever translates it), it means "so be it" or "yes, indeed." (The hip, contemporary "For sure!" is not a bad translation.) The New Testament, written in Greek, used the old Hebrew word, and with the same meaning. The people of the Bible used it exactly as we do. It implied a hearty "Yes!" to something that was said—roughly the same as saying, "I do" in a wedding ceremony. When Moses read the divine law to the Israelites, they said, "Amen" at various times. The word occurs several times in the praise songs of the Psalms. In a few places, the psalm writers got so caught up in their enthusiasm for God that they doubled the praise: "Amen and amen!" (see, for example, Psalm 41:13). The Jews came to use it as a word to express praise, and in the New Testament, Paul (a devout Jew before he became a Christian) used the word many times when he spoke of God.

A bit of trivia: Who is called "the Amen"? Jesus is. In Revelation 3:14 he refers to himself as "the Amen, the faithful and true witness, the ruler of God's creation." The key word here is "witness." As the faithful witness of God, Jesus himself is a "Yes!" to God.

We typically think of *amen* as an "ending word," since we're taught to end prayers that way. Not all prayers in the Bible end with an *amen,* although the most famous one (the Lord's Prayer) does. Several of the New Testament books end with an *amen,* including the last one, Revelation. In fact, it ends with a sort of "double amen": "Amen. Come, Lord Jesus. The grace of the Lord Jesus be with God's people. Amen" (Revelation 22:20-21).

DO I HAVE TO KNEEL?

Kneeling is the usual position for prayer, along with a bowing of the head. Is this the "Bible-approved" position? Yes and no. Yes, some people in the Bible got on their knees to pray. But we also read about people praying while standing (Jeremiah 18:20), sitting (2 Samuel 7:18), even lying face-down (Matthew 26:39). Some people prayed with hands lifted up, which is now becoming common again (1 Kings 8:22, 1 Timothy 2:80). People prayed silently (1 Samuel 1:13) and out loud (Ezekiel 11:13). They prayed alone (Matthew 6:6) and in groups (Acts 4:31). They prayed at scheduled times (Psalm 55:17) and at any time (Luke 18:1). They prayed in an open field (Genesis 24:11-12), in the temple (2 Kings 19:14), by a river (Acts 16:13), on a seashore (Acts 21:5), in bed (Psalm 63:6), and on a battlefield (1 Samuel 7:5).

Curiously, only one verse in the Bible even hints that people bowed their heads while they prayed: "King Hezekiah and his officials ordered the Levites to praise the LORD with the words of David and of Asaph the seer. So they sang praises with gladness and bowed their heads and worshiped" (2 Chronicles 29:30). Even in this verse, we aren't sure that bowing the head was actually connected with praying.

What about closing your eyes while praying? The Bible never mentions it. It doesn't mention placing your hands together, either.

The place, time, and posture are not emphasized in the Bible. The right attitude is. For the person who comes to God to praise him, to thank him, to ask for aid, or to confess sin, any posture is fine.

8

In a Nutshell:

ALL THE BOOKS OF THE BIBLE

· ·

As I already mentioned, I believe the Bible—the whole thing—is inspired by God. As a whole, it teaches us all we need to know about God, our relationship with him, and our destiny in this world and afterward.

What will you find in the different books of the Bible? That's what this chapter is about. A word of warning: Many books of the Bible aren't easily summarized in a few sentences. Nor is it easy to outline the books in the same way you could outline a magazine article or nonfiction book. The books of the Bible seem to "jump around," moving from one topic to another, not always with an immediately apparent sense of logic or a sense that the author had carefully *planned* the writing. In very few cases does it appear that the writer "thought things through" before writing.

But then, the Bible authors were writing as they were inspired by God. They weren't concerned with the rules of journalism or creative writing programs. They were not concerned about topic sentences, outlines, smooth transitions from one paragraph to the next. Thus the great book of Proverbs jumps from one topic to another, rather than lumping all the proverbs on marriage in one section, the proverbs on drunkenness in another, etc.

This doesn't mean the Bible authors weren't intelligent, or that they weren't good with words. They were. People have been reading their words for centuries, and they are still being read. But don't approach the Bible text expecting the type of organization you would find in, say, a home how-to book or a marriage manual. Some Bible books are more organized than others. In the New Testament, Matthew's Gospel is organized so that big concentrations of Jesus' teachings are found in special sections, alternating with other sections that focus on his miracles. Paul's letter to the Romans is a fairly well-organized summary of Christian beliefs. But Paul's other letters bounce around from one topic to another, the way we bounce around in conversations with old friends and frequently change the subject.

Through the rest of this chapter are brief summaries of each of the Bible's 66 books. Following each summary is a list of challenges you may encounter in reading the book. These lists are not intended to cast doubt on a book's worth. Knowing about the challenges before you encounter them can be helpful. Also helpful are some tips for recommended reading. These lists aren't intended to steer you away from any part of the Bible. Read the whole book if you can. But if you can't, knowing where the key parts are can help you to focus on the main aspects of a book.

The summaries here are presented in the same order that the books appear in the Bible. That doesn't mean I recommend you read the books in that order. For more information on a logical plan for Bible reading, see pages 114-30.

The Torah

Known as the Torah, the Law, the books of Moses, and the Pentateuch, the first five books are concerned with the world's beginnings and the birth of God's chosen nation, Israel. Tradition says the books were written or compiled by Moses, who is the chief character in all but the first (Genesis). For the Jewish religion, the first five books are *the* sacred books, more important than all other books, including the other books of the Old Testament. These five books are most often referred to by the Hebrew word *Torah,* which means "law"—or more accurately, "instruction." For Christians, their importance is that they show God as Creator and as one who provides people a moral law to guide them in this life. These books also show God making a covenant—a binding agreement—with Abraham and his descendants (the Hebrews). The agreement, basically, is this: "If you will obey me and be my law-abiding people, I will be your Guide and Protector in the world. When you abandon me and my law, and when you worship false gods, you will run into trouble."

Moses is the key figure here, and when the New Testament refers to the Bible's first five books, it uses phrases such as "Moses said" and "Moses wrote" and "Moses commanded." No other person in the Old Testament is viewed as having the authority Moses had. He was the great lawgiver and deliverer from Egypt, although in fact he is only the *human* leader, for it was God himself who revealed the law and led the people from Egypt.

The Torah were the first five books that the Hebrews/Jews accepted as being holy and authoritative. They are still the most studied and most honored among Jews today.

Much of what appears in the first five books is fascinating—the creation of the world, Abraham and his family, Jacob and his sons (the basis for a popular Broadway musical), the inspiring tale of Moses and the miraculous deliverance from the Egyptians (which made for a great movie with Charlton Heston). Yet some of the contents in these books leave people puzzled—most notably the page after page of rules, rules, rules. Most of these rules no longer apply today, such as the rules regarding animal sacrifices. But many of the rules about ethical dealings with each other still have value today. The Ten Commandments (found in Exodus 20 and Deuteronomy 5) are considered to be the high point of divine law in the Old Testament. If you remember nothing else from these five books, try to memorize the Ten Commandments.

Genesis

Summary: Genesis, in 50 chapters, deals with the world's beginnings. God creates the world, including man and woman. Man and woman fall into sin, but God promises salvation. The plan of salvation comes to focus on the tribe of Israel, descended from the patriarch Jacob and his 12 sons.

Genesis includes some of the best-known and most interesting characters and events in the Bible: Adam and Eve, Cain and Abel, Noah and the flood, the tower of Babel, Abraham, Isaac, and Jacob and sons, particularly the son Joseph. It is interesting reading throughout, and a knowledge of the book is essential for understanding the rest of the Bible. The book's title is the Greek word that means "beginnings" or "origins."

Challenges: One of the most fascinating documents in the world is, alas, the center of controversy, mostly because of questions about the nature of creation. Scoffers, armed with the data of science, snicker at the Genesis account of the world's and mankind's creation. These age-old controversies should have no effect on appreciating this remarkable book. (In fact, the Big Bang theory of the world's creation isn't radically different from Genesis' story of God creating the universe out of nothing.) Rather than getting caught up in the scientific controversies, readers should focus on the key teachings in the early chapters: God created the world from nothing. Man was made in God's image and was originally good. Man fell (and still falls) into sin because of his desire to be independent of God. These teachings in no way contradict science.

Recommendations for reading: You'll want to read pretty much the whole book. However, the "family tree" chapters (10, most of 11, 36, and most of 46) can be breezed through quickly.

Exodus

Summary: The tribe of Israel, enslaved in the Egyptian Empire, is led to freedom by the power of God, whose spokesman is the great figure Moses. An Israelite raised in the Egyptian court, Moses faces off with the formidable Pharaoh. God sends plagues on Egypt, and Pharaoh frees the Israelites, only to pursue them later. The Egyptian forces are drowned in the Red Sea. Once out of Egypt, Moses receives the Ten Commandments and other decrees from God. The freed Israelites prove to be a cantankerous and thankless mob as they progress toward their promised homeland in Israel. The book's title is a Greek word that means "going out."

Challenges: Did the plagues really happen? An open-minded person, aware of the wonders regularly being discovered by scientists, would answer, "Why not?" Even if they can be explained as natural phenomena, the faith question remains: Couldn't God have acted through natural means? The Israelites at that period in history would not have drawn a hard line (as we do today) between the natural and the supernatural, because they believed God controlled all natural processes. One passage that puzzles almost everyone is Exodus 4:21-26. This is one of the Bible's most notorious "fish bones." (See pages 100-03 for an explanation of "fish bones" in the Bible, and this one bone in particular.)

Recommendations for reading: Chapters 21–40 are mostly regulations for worship. However, they do contain some enlightening examples of moral instruction.

Leviticus

Summary: The book consists mostly of rules—for worshipping God, offering sacrifices, and handling everyday problems concerning cleanliness. The laws of kosher are contained here. The book's title refers to the Levites, Israel's tribe of priests. Moses was from this tribe. (Oddly, this book named for the Levites actually mentions them only once, in 25:32).

Challenges: The book's detailed description of animal sacrifices will repel some readers. Readers need to understand, though, that animal sacrifice has played a role in most major world religions, and in some areas it still does. You also need to have some understanding of the basic concept of offering a sacrifice in order to restore a right relationship with God.

Recommendations for reading: While the many rules might not seem interesting, chapter 19 contains some interesting laws about social ethics. Chapter 11 is somewhat interesting because it is the basis of the Jewish kosher foods laws. Chapter 16 lays down the rules for the Day of Atonement, which Jews still observe. This chapter is the origin of the concept of the "scapegoat." Chapter 23 lays down the rules for the other Jewish holy days. This is pretty important, since Jews still observe these days today, and these days play an important role later in the New Testament.

Numbers

Summary: Having left Egypt, the nation of Israel is still on its way through the wilderness to its homeland. The book is largely concerned with the people's rebellions against their God-appointed leaders and with God's miraculous provisions for the people's needs. Numbers also has several chapters of worship regulations. The book's title refers to the censuses of Israel (chapters 1 and 26), although a lot more happens in the book besides census-taking.)

Challenges: Some people might question the miracles described

"EYE FOR AN EYE"...PROGRESSIVE MORALS?

Yes, the idea of an eye for an eye, a tooth for a tooth really is in the Bible: "If anyone injures his neighbor, whatever he has done must be done to him: fracture for fracture, eye for eye, tooth for tooth. As he has injured the other, so he is to be injured" (Leviticus 24:19-20).

This law from the Old Testament strikes us as spiteful and vindictive. In the New Testament, Jesus taught a higher ethic: "You have heard that it was said, 'Eye for eye, and tooth for tooth.' But I tell you, Do not resist an evil person. If someone strikes you on the right cheek, turn to him the other also" (Matthew 5:38-39). Doesn't that sound better?

For the record, the Old Testament law was pretty compassionate and progressive. "Eye for eye, tooth for tooth" was a *limit.* It meant "tit for tat," but no more. When it comes to vengeance, many people want to get *more* than even. But the enlightened law in Leviticus said no, if you're injured you can't take two teeth because you lost one tooth. It was actually a progressive law. In light of that, we can imagine how the Bible authors would probably view personal injury lawsuits today.

in the book—for example, the miraculous provision of manna and quail for the Israelites. These are not challenges for any who accept the possibility of miracles. Perhaps a greater problem is the book's attitude toward non-Israelites, which seems hostile, to say the least. Keep in mind that, in Jewish and Christian tradition, God's salvation plan involved settling the Israelites in their promised homeland. Any individuals or nations who opposed this were, in effect, opposing God's will.

Recommendations for reading: As with Leviticus, the "rule" chapters can be skipped (7–10; 15; 18–19; 28–30). So can the chapters accounting the Israeli censuses and other lists (chapters 1–5; 26; 33–36). The story of Balaam and his talking donkey in chapter 22 is one that most people enjoy. By all means, read about the famous priestly blessing in 6:22-27. And read about the miraculous flocks of quail and the rebellion against Moses in chapters 11–12.

Deuteronomy

Summary: On the threshold of the Promised Land, Moses addresses the Israelites and reiterates much of the law (including the Ten Commandments) from the earlier books. He encourages Israel to follow God's law faithfully. Moses dies and is buried by God. The book's title means "second law," since it repeats many rules given earlier.

Challenges: As with Numbers, Deuteronomy takes a strong view toward non-Israelites, which contrasts with the New Testament's emphasis on love for one's enemies. The view reflects the Hebrews' belief in keeping their religion pure, which meant not accepting the ways of the heathen nations around them. Some of the practices of the other nations—such as child sacrifice and ritual prostitution—were truly horrible.

Recommendations for reading: Many of the rule chapters could be skipped (12–29). However, considering how often Deuteronomy is quoted in the New Testament (Jesus himself quoted it more than once), this important book deserves a good read-through at some point. Be sure to read about the consequences of obeying and disobeying God (chapter 28) and the story of Moses' death (chapter 34). Most people are touched by this depiction of the great leader who led his people to their new homeland but died before they entered this land. The chapter reveals the Hebrews' deep reverence for Moses.

The Historical Books

There is much history in the first five books of the Bible, but because they are so full of regulations, these books are often called "the Law." The books that follow are more directly concerned with historical events. Oddly, the Jews consider the books from Joshua through 2 Kings to be "the former prophets," using the term *prophets* not in the sense of those who predict, but those who reveal God's will to humankind. Several of these prophets—notably Samuel in 1 Samuel and Elijah in 1 Kings—are important figures in the Old Testament.

These books continue the story begun in the Law: Led out of Egypt by Moses, the Israelites now settle in their promised homeland, Canaan. Doing so involves driving out the heathen inhabitants who already live there. This violent process takes a long time, and the Israelites are constantly tempted to follow these people in their idolatrous worship practices (involving child sacrifice and other horrors). Even after the military leaders (called *judges*) secure peace for the Israelites, the people still go astray, forgetting that God gave them the land after freeing them from slavery in Egypt.

Following the lead of the neighboring nations, the people of Israel ask God for a single leader, a king. The first king, the great military leader Saul, begins well but ends as a failure. The second, David, becomes one of the great heroes of Hebrew history, second only to Moses in reputation. David's story and personal life are told in more detail than anyone else's. He is succeeded by his wise and wealthy son Solomon.

After Solomon's death, the kingdom of Israel splits into two nations—the southern kingdom, known as Judah, and the northern kingdom, still known as Israel. Both nations and their kings constantly lapse into idol worship and forget God. Both nations find themselves as pawns in the international power games of empires such as Egypt, Assyria, and Babylon. Israel is, generally, even more heathenized than Judah, and Israel is the first to fall to a heathen power (Assyria). Judah lingers on a bit longer but is finally conquered by Babylon. The leading people of Judah are then taken into exile in Babylon. The authors of the historical books assure the reader that all this occurred because the people would not keep the agreement to worship God alone. They neglected him, worshipped other gods, depended on foreign powers instead of God's power, and in the end, they paid the price.

The small book of Ruth is set in the period of the judges, and in our Bibles, it follows the book of Judges. In the Hebrew Bible, however, Ruth is part of the group of books known as the Writings (more on this later).

When you read the historical books, try not to focus on the minute details. The authors weren't giving information to prepare you for a quiz on names and dates. They were interested in God and his relation to people, particularly the nation of Israel. Focus on the forest, not the individual trees. The forest is this: God shaping rebellious people into a people of faith.

Joshua

Summary: Joshua, Moses' successor as leader of the Israelites, leads the settlement of the people into Canaan, the land given by God to Israel. Key events are the conquests of Jericho (with the tumbling walls) and Ai. The book (named, obviously, for its main human character) is essentially a story of conquest, a process that would have been impossible without God's help.

Challenges: As with earlier books in the Old Testament, Joshua paints a harsh picture of non-Israelites. But the picture is in keeping with the divine plan for establishing the true faith. Israel had no choice but to reject the grossly immoral beliefs and worship of the pagan inhabitants of Canaan.

Recommendations for reading: Some of the "list" chapters can be skipped (12–21). Much of the book is concerned with how the 12 tribes of Israel divided the land of Canaan among themselves. One wonderful and dramatic story is that of the fall of Jericho in chapter 6.

Judges

Summary: After Israel's settlement in Canaan, the people are periodically harassed by the neighboring nations. A series of judges arise to help conquer the enemies. *Deliverers* or *champions* would be more accurate terms, since they aren't judges in our modern legal sense. They are judges in the sense that they bring justice to the people by getting their enemies off their backs. Settled in Canaan, the Israelites repeatedly fall into the worship of false gods, which inevitably leads to disaster. Three of the Bible's most colorful characters, Samson the strongman, Jephthah, and Gideon, are key actors in the story. The woman judge, Deborah, is also an important figure.

Challenges: The book paints a painfully realistic picture of these violent and immoral times. Blood flows freely in the book, and even some of the heroes, such as Samson, engage in some morally questionable acts (consorting with a prostitute, for example). This shows what happens when people fail to follow God and fall away from him into the worship of false gods.

Recommendations for reading: Chapters 17–21, the book's closing section, are rather gruesome. The stories of the key judges are contained in the earlier chapters. Don't skip Gideon (6–8) or Samson (13–16). The book's last verse painfully summarizes the key theme of the whole book.

Ruth

Summary: Ruth, a woman in the neighboring nation of Moab, marries an Israelite man. Widowed, she leaves Moab with her Israelite mother-in-law, settles in Israel, and marries an Israelite. She becomes an ancestor of the famous King David.

Challenges: None—the book is a lovely story of a woman's devotion to her mother-in-law and her embracing of the faith of Israel.

Six books in the Old Testament were originally just three. First and 2 Samuel, 1 and 2 Kings, and 1 and 2 Chronicles were originally just Samuel, Kings, and Chronicles. Because they were so large and bulky in the form of scrolls, they were each divided in two.

Recommendations for reading: With only four chapters, this sweet tale can be read in 15 minutes. Considering it is set in the same violent period as the book of Judges, it is blissfully calm and blood-less—a nice relief if you've just finished reading Judges.

1 Samuel

Summary: The boy Samuel is called to God's service. When an adult, he serves as leader and judge of Israel. Oppressed by the Philistines, the people of Israel cry out for a warrior leader, and Samuel anoints Israel's first king, the handsome and militaristic Saul. But Saul proves to have some personal weaknesses, and God later chooses a better man, David. Much of the book concerns the rivalry between Saul and David. The book ends with Saul's death in a battle with the Philistines.

Challenges: In telling the story of the fascinating character David, the book seems to present two versions of how he came into the ser-vice of King Saul (chapters 16 and 17). However, the two accounts can be easily reconciled.

Recommendations for reading: The entire book is great reading, with great stories about God calling the boy Samuel, David slaying Goliath, David's close friendship with Jonathan, and Saul using the witch of Endor to summon Samuel's ghost. Some readers may want to skim quickly through the accounts of the battles with the Philistines.

2 Samuel

Summary: David laments Saul's death. After a brief war between his followers and those of Saul, David becomes king over all Israel. He makes Jerusalem the capital city. (This choice of Jerusalem as the Jewish capital still has an impact on affairs in the Middle East today.) Although devoted to God, David commits adultery, and his various children (by several wives) engage in incest, murder, and rebellion against the king. David reigns a long time, but endures many setbacks.

Challenges: The book is blunt in its descriptions of adultery, incest, court intrigue, and bloodshed. While David is an admirable character in many ways, his failings are described in painful detail. The book is an object lesson in the problems associated with the ancient practice of polygamy. It is clear that "blended families" had problems even in Bible times!

Recommendations for reading: Most of the book is interesting, particularly the parts covering David's family affairs. Some of the battles and rebellion accounts (chapters 10, 20, 21, 23, and 24) can be read through quickly.

1 Kings

Summary: King David dies, and some of his sons compete for the throne. His chosen successor, Solomon, eventually triumphs, and he establishes a reputation for wisdom. He also becomes the great builder of Israel, putting up the magnificent temple and other public buildings in Jerusalem. However, his many pagan wives (most of whom he marries for political alliances) lead him into idolatry. After his death, 10 of Israel's 12 tribes rebel against his son Rehoboam, and afterward there are two separate kingdoms: Israel (10 tribes) and Judah (2 tribes, ruled by David's descendants). The later chapters alternate between the two kingdoms. The fiery prophet Elijah is a major player, working to lead Israel back to worship of the true God. His adversaries, nasty King Ahab and the equally vile Queen Jezebel, are also key players.

Note: 1 and 2 Kings are said to draw on some long-vanished court histories—such as "the book of the annals of Solomon" and "the book of the annals of the kings of Israel."

Challenges: Many of the events in 1 and 2 Samuel and 1 and 2 Kings are retold in 1 and 2 Chronicles. There are some minor disagreements in the parallel accounts, none of which are of great importance.

Recommendations for reading: The accounts of the erecting of the temple and other buildings (chapters 5–8) can be read through very quickly (but read closely the temple prayer, 8:22-61). Beginning with chapter 14, the alternating accounts of the kings of Judah and Israel can be read quickly. But give full attention to the Elijah stories beginning at chapter 17. He is one of the key figures in the Old Testament, one who is mentioned several times in the New Testament. For the people of Israel, Elijah became the symbol of the true prophets of God.

2 Kings

Summary: As in the later chapters of 1 Kings, the book alternates between accounts of the two kingdoms of Judah and Israel. The prophet Elijah is miraculously taken to heaven, and his successor, the prophet Elisha, works many miracles. Most of the kings of Israel, and some kings of Judah, prove to be idol worshippers, but a few try to lead the people back to worshipping the true God. Eventually the kingdom of Israel is conquered by the Assyrian Empire. The kingdom of Judah is threatened by the Assyrians but is delivered by God. However, Judah is later conquered by the Babylonian Empire, and the country's ruling class is taken to exile in Babylon. The people of both Israel and Judah are punished for neglecting their duties to God.

Challenges: As with 1 Kings, some of the stories in 2 Kings do not totally agree with the stories told in 1 and 2 Chronicles. None of the points of disagreement are important. Some of the miracles of the prophet Elisha may seem unusual to the modern reader. It is interesting that in 1 and 2 Kings, the stories of Elijah and Elisha are almost the only ones containing miraculous elements.

Recommendations for reading: Many of the accounts of the various kings can be read quickly, but do attempt to read the entire book through at least once. Focus particularly on the reformer kings

Jehu (chapters 9–10), Hezekiah (18–20), and Josiah (22–23). The concluding chapter, giving the whole book's moral, is important to read.

The Writings

The books Joshua through 2 Kings tell history. So do 1 Chronicles through Esther. But the Jews have always put Chronicles, Ezra, Nehemiah, and Esther in a separate category known as the Writings—which also includes Job, Psalms, Proverbs, Ecclesiastes, the Song of Solomon, Ruth, Daniel, and Lamentations. In Jewish tradition, these writings are considered sacred, but they are not studied or honored in the same way as the Law, or the Bible's first five books.

First, consider the Writings that are historical in nature: 1 Chronicles, 2 Chronicles, Ezra, Nehemiah, and Esther. These tell the story of Israel from the reign of David down to the time when some Jews were still living in exile in Persia (as in Esther) while others had returned to resettle the land of Israel (as in Ezra and Nehemiah). The books of Joshua, Judges, 1 and 2 Samuel, and 1 and 2 Kings tell Israel's story, interpreted by authors who see the events as the working out of God's purposes in history. (By the way, the small book of Ruth, though it follows Judges in our Bibles, is considered part of the Writings.)

Second, some books in the Writings are more literary in nature. These include: Job, Psalms, Proverbs, Ecclesiastes, and Song of Solomon. They are some of the most-loved and most-read books in the Bible. These books are not historical (although Job tells, in poetic form, the "history" of the suffering of Job). They are poems (Psalms), advice (Proverbs), speculation about the meaning of life (Ecclesiastes), and a celebration of the pleasures of man and woman together (Song of Solomon).

The Writings were the last group of books that the Jews accepted as being holy and authoritative. However, the Jews (and Christians, also) have always loved and honored the book of Psalms, which both groups consider to be a high point of the Old Testament.

1 Chronicles

Summary: The book begins by listing the genealogy from Adam to King David. Beginning at chapter 10, it covers much of the same ground as 1 and 2 Samuel, beginning with the death of Saul and focusing on David's reign. Many of the more sordid details of David's life are excluded from 1 Chronicles. In some ways, 1 Chronicles is the cleaned-up, G-rated version of David's story.

Note something new in 1 and 2 Chronicles: the first case of a book of the Bible using other books as sources. It is obvious that the author(s) of Chronicles freely used materials from 1 and 2 Samuel and 1 and 2 Kings.

Challenges: The David we encounter here is a more idealized figure than the all-too-human David of 1 and 2 Samuel. It is the same man, but some of his failings are not mentioned. First Chronicles also differs in some minor historical details.

Recommendations for reading: The chapters of lists and genealogies (1–9; 12; 15; 18; 23–27) can be skipped. Generally speaking, the stories of David's life are told in more detail in 1 and 2 Samuel.

2 Chronicles

Summary: David's son Solomon reigns and builds the Lord's temple in Jerusalem. Ten of the 12 tribes rebel, forming the new kingdom of Israel (the two remaining tribes being called Judah). Unlike 1 and 2 Kings, 2 Chronicles gives almost no attention to the kingdom of Israel. Most of the later chapters cover the same ground as the accounts of Judah in 1 and 2 Kings. Judah is conquered by the Babylonians. The book ends with the promise of Cyrus, the Persian emperor, to let the people of Judah return to their homeland.

Challenges: As with 1 Chronicles, the book does not agree in all its historical details with the accounts in 1 and 2 Kings (which are probably older, and perhaps more accurate). However, none of the disagreements are important. The book seems to take a great interest in details about worship in the Jerusalem temple—details that probably interest few readers today.

Recommendations for reading: Most of this same material is covered in 1 and 2 Kings. However, the earlier chapters dealing with Solomon are more unique.

Ezra

Summary: The people of Judah are allowed to return from their exile in Babylon. Cyrus (whose empire, Persia, conquered the Babylonians) allows this return. Cyrus' successor takes an interest in the Jews' rebuilding of the temple and other structures. The new temple is built and dedicated. Ezra, a priest, comes with a second wave of exiles and helps the people focus on true worship of God, which includes rejecting the religious practices of neighboring nations. Ezra specifically forbids the marriage of Jews with non-Jews—an interesting development, since King Solomon had allowed his non-Jewish wives to lead him away from worshipping the one true God.

Challenges: Bible scholars have some difficulties pinning accurate dates on the events in the books of Ezra and Nehemiah. None of these historical issues is of any real concern to the nonscholar. The nonscholar may be more concerned about the book's attitude toward non-Jews. This attitude is understandable, considering that the nation of Judah had been conquered as a punishment for abandoning the worship of the one true God. Ezra was concerned that the people never again lapse into worshipping the false gods of the surrounding nations.

Recommendations for reading: This book has many lists and genealogies you can skip (chapter 2, most of chapter 8, and most of chapter 10). However, Ezra is an important character in the Old Testament and a good example of a spiritual and moral reformer.

Nehemiah

Summary: Nehemiah, a Jew, gives up his comfortable job as steward to the Persian king. He goes to Jerusalem and becomes governor of the Jews who have returned from Babylonian exile. He leads the settlers in repairing the city walls while facing opposition from nearby tribesmen. The priest Ezra is a key player in the story.

Challenges: Historians and Bible scholars have some difficulty fixing dates on the events in Ezra and Nehemiah. None of these problems is of any real concern to most Bible readers.

Recommendations for reading: Like 1 and 2 Chronicles and Ezra, Nehemiah has many "list" chapters (7; 10–11; most of 12).

Esther

Summary: The Persian king Ahasuerus (Xerxes in some translations) gets rid of his impudent wife and replaces her with Esther, a Jewish girl. Keeping her ethnic background a secret, Esther helps thwart the anti-Jewish plots of Haman, a Persian official who has a deep grudge against the Jews. Esther is aided by her relative, Mordecai. The Jews end up slaughtering the Persian henchmen who were pledged to kill them.

Challenges: The book never once mentions God or even prayer. It seems much more pro-Jewish than pro-God, and many historians have suggested it may just be a Jewish folk tale that serves to explain the Jewish feast of Purim. Though much treasured by Jews today (especially during their holiday of Purim), the book is never quoted or even mentioned in the New Testament. However, the traditional Christian view is that the book shows how the Jews' God is in control of the nation's destiny—even if he is never mentioned by name. He works to preserve his people in the midst of great danger.

Recommendations for reading: With only ten chapters, this book can be easily read in one sitting.

Job

Summary: Job, a rich and righteous man, loses his wealth, his children, and his health as Satan attempts to prove to God that religious people love God only as long as life is going well. Job's three wise friends arrive to comfort him, but they end up insisting that his suffering must be the result of sin in his life. Job protests that this is not so, that he truly is innocent. God himself speaks to Job out of a storm, asking what right Job has to question the workings of the Almighty. The book ends with God restoring Job's health and fortune.

Challenges: The speeches of Job's fourth friend, Elihu (found in chapters 32–37), add nothing new to what the other three friends have already stated. Some scholars think the Elihu chapters were a later addition to the book. (If you skip from the end of chapter 31 to the beginning of 38, you'll notice that the transition still reads quite smoothly.)

Recommendations for reading: While the Elihu chapters don't seem to add much new material to the book, Job is one of the most beautiful books in the entire Bible, dealing with one of life's most painful questions: Why do good people suffer? The answer hits home forcefully: We don't know why. We must trust that God, who controls everything, will be just. Job's speeches, and those of his three friends, express important ideas about justice in God's world. The book gives a hint (in 19:25) that perhaps justice has to occur in the next world, not in this one.

Psalms

Summary: The longest book in the Bible is not divided into chapters as is the rest of the Bible. Rather, it is 150 individual psalms, which are poems (or songs) expressing praise, worship, gratitude, anguish, or repentance. Written by a number of different authors over hundreds of years, they are the "hymnal" of the Old Testament. Of the 150, 73 are attributed to King David, famous in Israel as a "sweet singer." Of the David psalms, some of the most famous are chapters 23 (the Shepherd psalm) and 51 (the great song of sin and repentance).

Challenges: Many of the psalms seem to have an un-Christian (maybe we should say *pre*-Christian) attitude toward one's enemies. "Love your enemies," a key teaching in the New Testament, does not seem to be a guiding factor in the Psalms. Several call for God's wrath to fall upon the enemy. However, take these psalms at their face value: not as a description of the attitude we *ought* to have toward our enemies, but as an acknowledgment that God's justice eventually will be done. The "vengeance psalms" reflect the feelings of a deeply oppressed soul crying out to God. They are feelings we have all felt.

Recommendations for reading: All the psalms should be read, but not at one sitting because this is a long book. Since most of the psalms are no longer than a page, the practice of reading one per day is feasible. The longest psalm (119) is also the longest chapter in the entire Bible.

Some highlights are psalms 9, 19, 23 (the Shepherd psalm), 24, 37, 42, 46, 49, 51 (the great song of repentance), 86, 90, 100, 103, 130, 139 (beautiful), and 145.

Proverbs

Summary: This book is a collection of wise sayings, of good advice about how to conduct one's life. The various sayings focus on money, friendship, family, marriage, justice, wisdom and folly, and social behavior. While Psalms focuses on the relationship between God and man, Proverbs focuses on inter-human relations. However, God is never far from the author's mind, for "the fear of the LORD is the beginning of knowledge" (1:7). The proverbs are attributed to several authors, most notably the wise king of Israel, Solomon. It is one of the more practical books in the entire Bible, and even unbelievers have admired the book's wisdom.

Challenges: The book may give the impression that life will always go well for the wise and religious man—something that the book of Job obviously contradicts. Much of the book has a "this-worldly" orientation that bothers some people. It shouldn't, since there is no reason a spiritual person can't also be a practical person.

The description of the ideal wife (31:1-25) may strike some feminists as being outdated. Yet many women find it appealing.

Recommendations for reading: Like Psalms, Proverbs isn't meant to be read straight through at one sitting. And like Psalms, the whole book is important. This is great stuff, as even unbelievers have admitted over the centuries.

Ecclesiastes

Summary: The "Teacher" (or "Preacher" in some translations) reflects on the emptiness and meaningless of the things people pursue for happiness—pleasure, wisdom, wealth, fame. All these things have value only if God is at the center of man's existence. Man's duty is to obey God's commands. The book's title means "things said before the assembly." Tradition says the author was the wise king Solomon—a man who had wisdom, wealth, and power, but who learned that they do not bring true satisfaction to one's life.

Challenges: Ecclesiastes has a rather pessimistic tone, but the tone is in keeping with the book's theme: Most of the goals people pursue in life are a total waste of time. The book's structure puzzles many people; it doesn't seem to follow a logical line of thought, but rather skips around from one topic to another. But the whole book points to the main conclusion: Honoring God and keeping his commandments is the only way to a meaningful life.

Recommendations for reading: All 12 chapters are fascinating, though occasionally puzzling.

Song of Solomon

Summary: A man and woman in love sing of their deep feelings for each other. They praise each other's physical charms in extravagant poetry.

Challenges: Like the book of Esther, this book never once mentions God or anything even remotely spiritual. For this reason, both Jews and Christians have tended to interpret the book as symbolic—that is, the two lovers represent God and his people, bound together in deep love. The obvious truth is that the book, attributed to the wise king Solomon, is a collection of love poetry. (Since Solomon had hundreds of wives and concubines, it is a subject he should have known quite well.) The Song provides a nice antidote to the idea that religious people are anti-sex and anti-body.

Recommendations for reading: If you choose to read the book, it is short and quite interesting. It reminds us that God has no problem with genuine human love and physical attraction. The book can easily be read in ten minutes.

The Major Prophets

In the Christian Bible, the category of Major Prophets includes Isaiah, Jeremiah, Lamentations, Ezekiel, and Daniel. (The Jews place Lamentations and Daniel in the group known as the Writings.) We agree that Isaiah, Jeremiah, and Ezekiel are major because their books are long and, in terms of spiritual impact, very influential. Isaiah is one of the most-quoted books of the Bible, and Jeremiah and Ezekiel are not far behind. Christians are especially fond of the Major Prophets because many of their proclamations were fulfilled in the life of Jesus.

The prophets provide some balance in the Old Testament. The five books of the Law (Genesis through Deuteronomy) almost give the impression that being a good person means following a lot of ceremonial rules. The prophets made it clear that people could be technically law-abiding but still be unjust, oppressive, and spiritually corrupt. The prophets were "exposers"—men who showed that beneath an outward respectability, people could still be far from God. They were a sort of combination of preacher and journalist, uncovering immorality and proclaiming their warning far and wide so that people would (they hoped) see their errors and change their ways. The prophets were, in a sense, alarmists who cried out, "Warning! There's a moral and spiritual crisis here! Do something...quick!"

Isaiah

Summary: The prophet Isaiah, ministering in the kingdom of Judah, warns the people that they will be judged because of their wickedness. Beginning in chapter 40, he offers comfort and predicts that the exiles in Babylon will return home. He also anticipates a "suffering servant" of God, a savior who will bring deliverance. He says that one day, God will set up a new and righteous kingdom.

Challenges: Bible scholars debate the obvious change that occurs between chapters 39 and 40. The tone and language of the book change dramatically, and some scholars believe there were two Isaiahs (one who was the source of chapters 1–39, and another who wrote chapters 40–66). The first part of Isaiah is mostly warnings about coming disaster, while the second part is a more gentle word of consolation. Most Bible readers have nothing to gain from getting caught up in this controversy; the entire book has inspired people for centuries.

Recommendations for reading: Isaiah is one of the most loved books in the Bible. It is quoted or referred to frequently in the New Testament. While it is long (66 chapters), and much of the material deals with relations with ancient empires, the whole book focuses on the need for people to rely on God alone. The book is especially interesting because many of Isaiah's words seem to be fulfilled in the life and work of Jesus. Definitely do *not* skip Isaiah's commission (chapter 6), the predictions of a Messiah (9; 11; 42; 49), and the words of comfort (40; 43). The warnings against ancient empires can be read through quickly (15–23).

Jeremiah

Summary: Jeremiah, called to be a prophet while a young man in the kingdom of Judah, preaches during the reign of good king Josiah. Later kings despised Jeremiah for his dire words of warning, and much of the book concerns Jeremiah's sufferings at the hands of his political enemies. Jeremiah predicts a "new covenant" between

BOOK BURNING?

Christians—and some people who oppose Christians—have been accused of being book-burners. The first book-burner was wicked King Jehoiakim. Warming himself by a fire in the palace in Jerusalem, Jehoiakim received a scroll from the prophet Jeremiah. While an aide read from the scroll (which had nothing good to say for the nasty monarch), Jehoiakim sliced off the portion just read and tossed it into the fire. He continued until the entire scroll had been burned (Jeremiah 36:21-23).

God and man, which Christians say was fulfilled with the coming of Jesus. After Jerusalem's destruction by the Babylonians, Jeremiah stays with the group that remains in the land. Eventually he flees with a group of Jewish people who go to Egypt.

Challenges: Jeremiah's prophecies are not in chronological sequence, so it is hard to read the book without a familiarity with Judah's history (found in 2 Kings and 2 Chronicles).

Recommendations for reading: This much-loved, much-quoted (and long) book deserves a slow, steady read-through. Jeremiah was a sensitive soul, painfully aware that his country had turned its back on God and was about to pay the price for its sins. The prophecies against ancient nations (chapters 46–51) may make for difficult reading.

Lamentations

Summary: The author (who may have been the prophet Jeremiah) grieves over the Babylonians' destruction of the holy city, Jerusalem. He recognizes that the Jews brought the calamity on themselves, and that God's love still endures for his people.

Challenges: None, except that the tradition that Jeremiah wrote the book is sometimes doubted. The book itself does not name its author. It is probably an accurate reflection of Jeremiah's feelings at seeing Jerusalem in ruins.

Recommendations for reading: This brief book of sad poetry can be read in a short time. It is sad but comforting, since it conveys the message that God is still in control, in spite of hardships.

Ezekiel

Summary: The author, a Jew living in exile in Babylon, sees visions of God in his majesty. Ezekiel explains to the exiled people why they suffered the destruction and deportation by the Babylonians: They brought it on themselves by their own sin. But Ezekiel promises that God will regather the Israelites from the ends of the earth and restore them to a new kingdom. The countries who oppose this will be defeated. One of Ezekiel's key messages is that God is the divine

Judge of all people, but that he takes no pleasure in punishing the wicked. God, who is loving and forgiving, is eager to pardon the repentant person. This theme, which occurs frequently in the Bible, sees its fulfillment in the New Testament in the life and teachings of Jesus.

Challenges: Ezekiel strikes some readers as an unusual book because of its many strange visions. Some have even suggested that Ezekiel was a psychotic, not a prophet from God. While it's true that Ezekiel's visions (as in chapter 1) are sometimes strange, their uniqueness *does* have the desired impact: They catch and hold the reader's attention. God, communicating to and through Ezekiel, was revealing his "otherness," his supernatural separateness from human beings, while at the same time drawing near to them to communicate. The vision of the dry bones is the most famous of Ezekiel's visions (chapter 37).

Recommendations for reading: Do *not* skip the key "vision" passages: chapters 1–5; 17; 37), nor the chapter on individual responsibility (18), on God's care (34), or on having a new heart (36). Some of the warnings against the nations could be bypassed (25–32; 35; 38–39). The closing chapters (40–48) describe God's restoration of the city of Jerusalem. The book's last verse packs a wallop.

Daniel

Summary: This book has two main sections. The first (chapters 1–6) tells the story of the young Israelite Daniel exiled in Babylon (and later in Persia). Living under pagan kings who persecute true believers, the golden boy Daniel remains steadfast and true. The second section (7–12) consists of visions of the "end times," visions similar to those in the New Testament's book of Revelation.

Challenges: Historians and scholars have cast some doubts on the truth of Daniel's story. The book mentions the Babylonian king Nebuchadnezzar going insane and living in the wilderness. While the king was definitely a historical figure, no other history of the times mentions Nebuchadnezzar's madness—a notable oversight.

On the other hand, we wouldn't necessarily expect the official Babylonian records to mention this embarrassing incident, would we?

King Belshazzar was doubted as being a real person until around 1854, when archaeologists found him named in some Babylonian histories. The historians say he wasn't actually a king, nor was he the son of Nebuchadnezzar, as the book of Daniel says. But the book may be using "son of" in a wider sense—that is, "descendant of." And "king" may be used in the broader sense of "ruler" or "official," not just "the one and only king."

Scholars have been arguing for years over the visions (chapters 7–12). Do the symbols in them refer to ancient empires or to events at the end of the world? We can't answer that here. Like the visions in the book of Revelation, they do carry the message that God, not the world's rulers, is in control of history and will eventually bring justice.

Recommendations for reading: Definitely read chapters 1 through 6, which include interesting (and familiar) stories of Nebuchadnezzar's dream of the statue, Daniel's friends in the fiery furnace, the ghostly handwriting on the wall at Belshazzar's feast, and, of course, Daniel in the lions' den. The visions in chapters 7 through 12 puzzle even the wisest of readers, but do note that 12:1-3 contains one of the few Old Testament statements about life after death, with heaven for some people and hell for others.

The Minor Prophets

Minor doesn't mean "unimportant," but rather, is used to distinguish these books from those found in the Major Prophets. Some of the Minor Prophets do seem minor to us, since their messages seem to apply only to the distant past (literally, ancient history). But some of them are still highly readable because of their teachings on the need for justice (notably Amos), God's willingness to forgive (notably Hosea), and the need for us to "keep the faith" even when injustice seems to rule in the world (Habakkuk). Some passages in the Minor Prophets are treasured by Christians because they predict certain events in the life of Jesus (Micah's prophecy of the Messiah being born in Bethlehem, for example).

The 12 books of the Minor Prophets were originally one book (scroll, that is) in the Hebrew Bible. This scroll was usually referred to as "the Twelve."

Hosea

Summary: Hosea is a prophet living in the kingdom of Israel (the northern kingdom, which had split from the southern kingdom, Judah, after King Solomon's death). The book often refers to the nation as *Ephraim,* which is the name of its largest piece of territory. The book uses Hosea's own experience with his unfaithful wife, Gomer, to illustrate God's love for the unfaithful kingdom of Israel. As Hosea forgives Gomer for chasing other men, so God will forgive Israel for worshipping other gods. Note that in the Old Testament, idolatry involves more than bowing down before statues. It means neglecting the true God, which inevitably results in mistreating other people as well.

Challenges: Some experts doubt that the chapters are in the right sequence, but this is not important to the average reader.

Recommendations for reading: Hosea is only 14 chapters, so read it all. It is a beautiful book about God's forgiveness.

Joel

Summary: The prophet Joel describes a plague of locusts, or crop-devouring grasshoppers. This is a symbol of judgment and destruction for those who neglect God. But Joel also predicts the coming of God's Holy Spirit on his people and warns of disaster for the nations that oppress Israel.

Challenges: Unlike some of the prophetic books, Joel does not open with any indication of the date. (Most of the books indicate their date by mentioning the reign of a specific king. Joel doesn't.)

Recommendations for reading: With only three chapters, this book can be read quickly. Note especially the prophecy of the Spirit in 2:28-32.

Amos

Summary: Here is a prophet for our times, the great advocate of justice. Amos, a simple shepherd in the northern kingdom of Israel, warns the Israelites that the injustice heaped on people, especially the poor, would bring doom on the nation. For those who live rightly, God will restore the kingdom. Among the 12 minor prophets, Amos is often considered the most practical. His words about oppressing the poor make the book easy for modern readers to relate to.

Challenges: None. Amos is one of the best-preserved books in ancient manuscripts.

Recommendations for reading: Chapters 1 and 2 can be skimmed quickly, since they are warnings against the sins of neighboring nations. You will want to read the rest of the book, where Amos warns the Israelites against trampling the poor (5:11) and other social sins. Note especially the warning (5:18-27) against people who appear religious on the outside but take advantage of others.

Obadiah

Summary: Obadiah, only one chapter in length, prophesies doom for Israel's neighboring nation, Edom. It had invaded and plundered Jerusalem four times, and Obadiah predicted its comeuppance. (His prophecy was later fulfilled; the Edomites are heard of no more after A.D. 70.)

Challenges: Although there are literally dozens of Obadiahs in the Bible, we don't know which one wrote this book. We also can't date the book with precision. These are unimportant problems.

Recommendations for reading: This book is so short, it should all be read.

Jonah

Summary: The Hebrew prophet Jonah is told by God to go to Nineveh, the capital of the Assyrian Empire, and preach against the people's wickedness. Jonah runs away by ship, is tossed overboard, and lands in a huge fish's belly. He is coughed up on land, goes to Nineveh to preach, and then is disgusted when the heathen people actually do repent. The message here has nothing to do with whales or fish, but with God's purpose for the world: He wants all people to repent, even those whom we perceive as heathen outsiders.

Challenges: No part of the Bible (except maybe the opening chapters of Genesis) causes more snickers among unbelievers than the book of Jonah. "Swallowed by a whale? Yeah, right." Well, scientifically speaking, people *have* survived after being swallowed by whales (and no doubt thought their survival was miraculous). The whale problem is a minor difficulty. Of more concern to some is that the account reads more like a folk tale than history. Why, for example, when the Bible takes such pains to record the names of foreign kings (Nebuchadnezzar, Sennacherib, etc.) does Jonah fail to mention the name of the king of Nineveh—even though that king repents and turns to God? Why have archaeologists yet to find mention of such a nationwide repentance? We can't answer these questions, except to say that acceptance of faith involves accepting God's miraculous intervention in human affairs. Rather than concentrating on the historical and scientific problems, consider the more important message: God loves not only his "chosen people" (the Hebrews), but all people. Jonah represents a chosen one who does not wish to share the message of divine love for all. God shows Jonah—vividly—that he shouldn't run away from preaching this message.

Curiously, of the 12 minor prophets, Jonah is the only one mentioned by Jesus. Jesus even refers specifically to Jonah's time in the sea creature's belly. So don't pass off this aspect of Jonah too quickly.

Recommendations for reading: Jonah is only four chapters long, and is easy to read. Pay careful attention to the message.

Micah

Summary: Living in Judah (the southern kingdom), Micah preaches God's judgment for his people's sins. They will be judged for oppressing the poor and living unholy lives. But the kingdom will be restored by God, and a ruler born in Bethlehem will build a kingdom that will last forever.

Challenges: None.

Recommendations for reading: Micah is only seven chapters long and is easy to read. Pay special attention to the prophecy of a king from Bethlehem (5:2, which points ahead to Jesus' birth in Bethlehem) and the famous statement about walking humbly with God (6:8).

Nahum

Summary: The cruel nation of Assyria will get its comeuppance, says Nahum. The nation and its capital, Nineveh, have oppressed many nations. But like all evil empires, it will fall, doomed to ruin. God decrees this, and his people can rejoice that justice will be done.

Challenges: We ought to read this book with the understanding that human oppressors, no matter how powerful they seem, are doomed. God did not intend that oppressive powers would endure forever.

Recommendations for reading: At only 3 chapters, the book can be read quickly.

Habakkuk

Summary: In a dialogue with God, Habakkuk raises some good questions: Why do wicked people seem to prosper? God replies that another nation, the Babylonians, will come and punish the wicked people of Judah. Habakkuk then asks God, "Why send a cruel and oppressive nation to punish us?" God answers that good people live by faith, and God will always do what is right. The book ends with a song of praise to God, a song similar to those found in Psalms.

Challenges: The prophet gives no information about the date of his writing, so we have no idea when the book was written. This is unimportant, since the book's message has eternal value.

Recommendations for reading: The book is only three chapters long and very readable.

Zephaniah

Summary: Like the other prophets, Zephaniah warns God's

people against pride and oppression. He predicts a "day of the
LORD" (1:15), a day of judgment. He also predicts that the oppressive neighboring nations will be destroyed.

Challenges: None.

Recommendations for reading: The warnings against the neighboring nations (2:4-15) can be skimmed quickly. Otherwise, the entire book is only three chapters long.

Haggai

Summary: The Persian king Darius allows the exiled Jews to return to their country. The prophet Haggai, part of the returning group, encourages Zerubbabel, the Jewish governor, in rebuilding the Jerusalem temple, which the Babylonians had wrecked many years before.

Challenges: None. This book is very clear about its date (520 B.C., precisely) and purpose.

Recommendations for reading: At only two chapters in length, this book can be read quickly.

Zechariah

Summary: Working at the same time as Haggai, Zechariah encourages those who are rebuilding Jerusalem at a time when they are ready to give up. His sermons include various visions—four horns, a flying scroll, etc. The book's second section (9–14) prophesies a coming Messiah, the final judgment, and a long-term kingdom.

Challenges: As in the book of Daniel, this book has two sections that are radically different (1–8; 9–14). This shouldn't concern the average reader.

Recommendations for reading: Chapters 1–8, concerning events in Zechariah's own time. The remaining chapters, prophesying events that seem to be fulfilled in the life of Jesus, should be read.

Malachi

Summary: Malachi, who prophesied after the time of Haggai

and Zechariah, warns the Jews who had returned from exile that their religious life is not what it should be. They were marrying foreign (that is, unbelieving) wives and neglecting God. Judgment will come, but for good people there is nothing to fear. Before the "day of the Lord" comes, God will send a great prophet.

Challenges: We don't know who Malachi was, and it is possible his name (which means "messenger") is just a title ("the Messenger"), and not his actual name.

Recommendations for reading: Some of the warnings about the temple and tithing (1:6–2:9; 3:6-12) seem unimportant to modern readers. However, the book is only four chapters long, and some of Malachi's prophecies (especially those in chapter 4) seem to be fulfilled in the New Testament. Note that the prediction of Elijah coming (4:5) was thought to be fulfilled with the coming of Jesus' relative, John the Baptist.

The Apocrypha

About 400 years separate the prophet Malachi (at the end of the Old Testament) and the birth of Jesus (the beginning of the New Testament). During this period, many things happened to the Jews' religion, morals, and politics. Much of it was recorded in the books we call the *Apocrypha*. Some Bibles include these books, while others do not. Why?

The Jews inherited the sacred writings of their Hebrew-Israelite ancestors. By the time Jesus was born, the Jews had pretty much accepted all the books that we now call the Old Testament. They had not officially accepted the books written during the period between the two Testaments. These books were read by the Jews, but they weren't as old as the Old Testament books and were not as widely respected. Some of the apocryphal books had been written in Hebrew, but even these had never been included in the Hebrew version of the sacred books.

The first Christians accepted the Jewish sacred writings as their own. But some weren't so sure about the Apocrypha. Some Christians noted that none of the apocryphal books was ever quoted by

Jesus or anyone else in the New Testament. Thus they doubted that the Apocrypha was inspired and authoritative in the way the Old Testament was.

When the great scholar Jerome translated the Old and New Testaments into Latin, he was living in Palestine, the Jews' old homeland. Conversations with the Jewish teachers there convinced him that the apocryphal books did not belong in the Bible. But his superiors pressured him to translate them anyway. He did, but reluctantly. They became part of the Vulgate, Jerome's Latin translation, Christianity's "official" Bible for hundreds of years. So for centuries after Jerome, the Apocrypha was part of all Bibles throughout Europe.

A change came with the Protestant Reformation in the 1500s. The Protestant leaders remembered Jerome's hesitancy about having the Apocrypha in the Bible. Didn't the Jews exclude the Apocrypha from their Hebrew Bibles? So the new Protestant Bibles set the Apocrypha in a separate section of the Bible, indicating that it wasn't on par with the inspired books. The Catholic authorities reacted to the Protestants by issuing a decree that said the apocryphal books really are sacred Scripture. The great divide came in 1804, when the British and Foreign Bible Society, a very influential group, decided to drop the Apocrypha entirely. From that point on, almost all Protestant Bibles dropped the Apocrypha, while Catholic Bibles included it. That is still the case today. Some companies today publish Bibles with the Apocrypha, marketing it to both Catholics and Protestants. (To make matters even more complicated, the Eastern Orthodox churches accept part of the Apocrypha, but not all of it.)

The books of the Apocrypha are Tobit, Judith, the Wisdom of Solomon, Ecclesiasticus (don't confuse this with Ecclesiastes, a book in the Old Testament), Baruch, the Letter of Jeremiah, 1 and 2 Maccabees, and additions to the Old Testament books of Esther and Daniel. All Catholic Bibles include these books. Some of these, particularly Wisdom of Solomon (which is not by Solomon) and Ecclesiasticus, are full of wise sayings much like the Old Testament book of Proverbs.

If you are new to the Bible, it's probably wise to stick with the

Martin Luther, the great German leader of the Protestant Reformation in the 1500s, translated the entire Bible into German. He included the Apocrypha, but had some doubts about it. He placed it in a section between the Old and New Testaments and stated that these books were not equal to the holy Scriptures, but they were useful for reading. It was Luther who coined the term *Apocrypha,* which means "hidden things."

66 books in the Old and New Testaments. All Christians agree that these books are sacred, whereas there are (and probably always will be) some serious doubts about the Apocrypha.

One curious item about the Apocrypha: Its version of the book of Esther does mention God and prayer. The shorter book of Esther in the Protestant Old Testament does not.

The New Testament

You don't have to read very long to realize that the two Testaments are very different. Personal names, for example, are quite different. The action of the New Testament takes place in the Roman Empire, which used a form of Greek (called *koine,* "common") as its empire-wide language of trade and mass communication. (In a similar way, India today uses English as an official language in a nation that speaks hundreds of native Indian languages.) The Jews are now under Rome's political thumb. Rome is powerful and seems destined to stay. The Jews look in anticipation for the fulfillment of Old Testament prophecies about a king, a Messiah (meaning "anointed one"), who will lead the people to political, military, and spiritual freedom.

The authors of the writings that became the New Testament believed that this Messiah was Jesus Christ (*Christ* has the same meaning as *Messiah*). Jesus, however, was not a political leader but a spiritual leader. More than that, he became the mediator between God (loving, but angry at human sin) and man (sinful, unable to approach a holy God and have a relationship with him). This was what Jesus' followers, the Christians, believed. The Jews accused the Christians of preaching nonsense or a heretical form of Judaism that had no right to exist. But the Christians persisted, claiming that Jesus the Messiah had put them in a right relationship with God forever. Jesus, who was executed by crucifixion, rose up from the dead and ascended to heaven, and someday, all his followers would be raised up in the same way. And at the end of history, Jesus will bring this present world to a close and begin a new world with no sorrow or pain.

The Gospels and Acts

Gospel means "good news." The early Christians thought it was "good news" that Jesus, the Messiah, enabled people to live in a right relationship with God, a relationship that would endure beyond death.

In the early days of Christianity there were many Gospels. So how come only four made it into the Bible? The ones that didn't make it were often so ridiculous that we now wonder how anyone could have believed them. (For example, one had the boy Jesus making birds out of clay, clapping his hands, and bringing them to life.) Many of these fake Gospels were written by teachers pushing their own brands of strange philosophy or occult teaching and attempting to gain credibility by putting their words in the mouth of Jesus. These pseudo-Gospels were often circulated under the name of one of Jesus' apostles—the Gospel of Thomas, for example.

The fact is, the early Christians, over the course of time, came to agree that Matthew, Mark, Luke, and John were somehow *right*— that the Jesus they presented was the real Jesus, the one remembered by his followers.

Luke was also the author of the book of Acts, which tells of the activities of the earliest Christians.

Matthew

Summary: Through his legal father, Joseph, Jesus is descended from the faithful patriarch Abraham, the father of the Hebrew people. Jesus is born of the virgin Mary through the power of God's Holy Spirit. When he reaches adulthood, his relative John the Baptist is leading spiritual revivals and telling people to repent and turn to God. John baptizes Jesus, beginning Jesus' public ministry. The devil tempts Jesus to become a political Messiah and wonder-worker, but Jesus resists. Jesus calls a group of 12 disciples and goes throughout the country healing people of diseases and demon possession. He teaches people that the law in the Old Testament was good, but God is also concerned about people's inward attitude toward God and others. One of Jesus' key teachings is about the kingdom of heaven, meaning God's reign among human beings. Jesus tells many parables, or illustrations, of what this kingdom of heaven is like. Around the time of the Passover, the Jews' main religious festival, Jesus goes to Jerusalem. On the way he is hailed as the Jews' Messiah by many of the common folk. The Jewish religious authorities see him as a rebel and a threat to their position. One of Jesus' disciples, Judas Iscariot, arranges to hand Jesus over to the Jewish authorities. Jesus has a fellowship meal with his disciples (the Last Supper), then Judas arranges for his arrest. Jesus is tried before different courts, then by the Roman governor, Pilate. Pilate finds Jesus guilty of no crime, but under pressure from the Jews, he allows Jesus to be executed by crucifixion. Jesus dies on the cross and is buried. Afterward he rises from the dead and his tomb is found empty. He appears to his disciples and tells them to make new followers throughout the world. He promises he will always be with them.

Challenges: Matthew has no problems except that his story of Jesus' life and teachings don't agree in some small details with the stories in the other three Gospels (Mark, Luke, and John). Most of these details are very minor. If you have ever had to give a testimony in court, you know that different eyewitnesses (even if they're all intelligent and sensible people) can vary slightly in their descriptions of the same event.

Recommendations for reading: Matthew is one of the most quoted books in the Bible. Matthew is especially known as the "teaching" Gospel, full of Jesus' teachings on ethics and the spiritual life. Especially quotable are the Sermon on the Mount (chapter 5–7), the parables of the kingdom of heaven (13; 20), the "woes" against hypocrites (23), and the parables about being ready for God (25).

Mark

Summary: Mark is like a short version of Matthew. It omits Jesus' family tree and the story of his birth and goes right to his adult career. It also omits many (not all) of the parables and other teachings found in Matthew. Mark is a Gospel of action, with Jesus moving about frequently, healing the sick and demon-possessed. As in Matthew, Jesus is crucified and raised from the dead, but...

Challenges: Mark lacks an ending—or, looked at another way, we don't know for sure where it ends. Chapter 16, which tells of Jesus' empty tomb, breaks off suddenly. Some of Jesus' followers see that his tomb is empty, then suddenly there is a break in the ancient manuscripts. The break occurs at 16:8. Your Bible includes 16:9-19, which shows Jesus appearing to his disciples. This break puzzles the Bible scholars, since the oldest manuscripts discovered to date don't have 16:9-19. So is 16:9-19 the real ending, or was the original ending lost? We don't know. (Perhaps this is a reason to be glad we have four Gospels instead of one. What if we only had Mark?) Mark, by the way, is supposed to have been a friend of Peter, Jesus' disciple. So Mark's Gospel is based on the reports of a reliable eyewitness, Peter.

The ever-popular musical play *Godspell* bills itself as being "based on the Gospel according to St. Matthew."

Recommendations for reading: Everyone ought to read every word of all four Gospels. It's true, however, that Mark (which may be the first of the four Gospels to have been written) doesn't give us as much teaching as Matthew and Luke.

Luke

Summary: In many ways, Luke's Gospel is similar to Matthew's, though Luke arranges the material in different sequences. But Luke also includes some information that no other Gospel does—notably the Christmas story details about Jesus' mother Mary, Jesus' relative John the Baptist, and the birth of Jesus (including the angels and the shepherds) as found in chapters 1 and 2. Chapter 2 also includes the only story of the boy Jesus, who at age 12 amazes the religious authorities with his wisdom. Luke's Gospel, unlike Matthew's and Mark's, ends with Jesus being taken into heaven (known as the *ascension*).

Challenges: Again, Matthew, Mark, and Luke don't agree in every detail. But the differences are very minor.

Recommendations for reading: Well, you can read rather quickly through Jesus' genealogy in 3:23-38. But, like Matthew, Luke is a gem, even though it covers much of the same ground as Matthew. If you read Matthew closely (which you should), you could skip much of Luke. But do *not* skip the material that is found only in Luke's Gospel: the Christmas story (1–2), the miraculous catch of fish (5:1-11), the "woes" (6:24-26), the parable of the good Samaritan (10:29-32), the story of Mary and Martha (10:38-42), the parable of the rich fool (12:13-21), the parable of the prodigal son (15:11-32), the account of the rich man and Lazarus (16:19-31), the parable of the unjust judge (18:1-8), the story about the Pharisee and the tax collector (18:9-14), the story of Zacchaeus (19:1-10), Jesus' trial before Herod (23:6-16), the risen Jesus on the road to Emmaus (24:13-35), and Jesus' ascension into heaven (24:36-49).

John

Summary: John's Gospel, supposed to have been written by one of Jesus' disciples (John, naturally), is very different from the other three. While this is the same Jesus, John chooses to emphasize other miracles and other teachings. He begins not with Jesus' birth or public ministry, but before the world begins. According to John, Christ was "the Word," the revelation of God, who existed with

God before the world was made. In John's Gospel Jesus is also "the Lamb of God, who takes away the sin of the world" (1:29). This Jesus engages in some dialogues about being "born again" (in the heart, that is) in his famous encounter with Nicodemus (chapter 3) and about his being "living water" (chapter 4). In fact, John's Gospel is full of Jesus' "I am" statements: Jesus refers to himself as "the bread of life" (6:35), "the light of the world" (9:5), "the gate for the sheep" (10:9), "the good shepherd" (10:11), "the resurrection and the life" (11:25), "the way and the truth and the life" (14:6), "the true vine" (15:1), etc. Obviously John does not present Jesus as a ranting egomaniac. He says these things about himself because they are true. He is the Son of God, the Savior, and all these other things as well.

As in the other Gospels, Jesus is crucified, buried, then raised from the dead. John's Gospel includes some additional postresurrection stories, including the famous one about "doubting Thomas," the apostle who had to touch the resurrected Jesus' wounds before he would believe it was really Jesus and not a specter.

Challenges: John has no problems, except that it is different from (but doesn't really contradict) the other three Gospels. In John's Gospel, Jesus makes a lot of "I am" statements—"I am the vine," "I am the resurrection and the life," etc. Coming from an ordinary human being, these statements would be viewed as raw ego. But the authors of the Gospels believed Jesus was not just fully human, but also the Son of God—the one person who could make these amazing "I am" statements truthfully.

Recommendations for reading: Don't skip a word. John's Gospel is so rich that, like a hearty meal, it ought to be read slowly, savoring every word. Because it includes a lot of details that the other Gospels omit, it is important to study this fascinating document up close.

Acts

Summary: Luke continues his Gospel with the story of the early Christians, concentrating on some key apostles, notably Paul and Peter. Acts begins where Luke ends, with Jesus being taken up

The popular rock opera *Jesus Christ Superstar* is based on the Bible, but it offers an alternative view of Jesus' end. *Superstar* ends with a musical number called "John 19:41," which is this verse: "At the place where Jesus was crucified, there was a garden, and in the garden a new tomb, in which no one had ever been laid." The Jesus in *Superstar* is buried, but not raised from the dead. That is one reason the play aroused so much controversy among Christians, who believe Jesus did rise from the dead.

to heaven. A replacement disciple is found for Judas, who killed himself after betraying Jesus. At the Jewish festival of Pentecost in Jerusalem, the Holy Spirit comes, as Jesus predicted. The Spirit gives special power to the apostles. The early Christians engage in prayer and fellowship, and the apostles work miracles of healing. Like Jesus, they are jailed and harassed by the Jewish authorities, but the church continues to grow. Stephen, a faithful Jewish Christian, becomes the first Christian to die for his beliefs, stoned to death by an angry Jewish mob. Paul, a Jewish persecutor of Christians, becomes a Christian himself and becomes the most widely traveled apostle, preaching the gospel and starting new Christian communities among the Gentiles (non-Jews)—thus breaking Christianity out of its Jewish mold. The Jewish authorities feel threatened by Paul, and have him arrested and sent to Rome. There, while awaiting trial, Paul preaches the gospel even though he is under house arrest.

Challenges: None of any significance. Archaeologists have found that Luke "did his homework." The historical details of his book, including the people he mentions (Roman officials such as Felix and Festus, for example) have been verified as historically accurate.

Recommendations for reading: Read the whole book! Acts is wonderful and readable. It is a neglected part of the Bible, and it is almost the only eyewitness account of the first Christians. With executions, exorcisms, visions, arrests, martyrdoms, sorcerers, and shipwrecks, it is a colorful and dynamic book. It shows how the faith could spread in a world filled with a diverse mix of people, religions, and beliefs (not so different from our own world, in fact).

The Epistles

The words *epistle* and *letter* are the same, more or less. Actually, an epistle is kind of like a sermon on paper. The New Testament, from Romans to Jude, consists of epistles/letters from the early Christian leaders to Christian groups or individuals with instructions about Christian beliefs and behaviors.

People who are not familiar with the Bible may well ask, "Why are these *letters* so important?" They show us—vividly—what the early Christians believed, how they lived, and how they interpreted God's will for their lives. Later Christians accepted the letters as sacred writing, the instructions of the apostles to Christians everywhere. The letters were accepted as the authoritative writings of people who knew Jesus best—an important point, since Jesus himself wrote nothing.

The main letter-writer was Paul, the high-energy apostle who dominates the closing chapters of the book of Acts. Paul, a Jewish Christian, became the apostle to the Gentiles (non-Jews). His work among the Gentiles was decisive, since it spread Christianity beyond its Jewish roots into a global faith that could be exported to any land and any group of people regardless of their religious background. With Paul, Christianity became a universal faith. In the letters, Paul dealt frequently with misconceptions about the Christian faith. For example, he constantly fought against *legalism,* the attitude (common among Jews of his day) that we can gain our salvation by obeying rules, or "racking up points with God." According to Paul's

The New Testament is a Christian book, but the word *Christian* appears in it only three times. Its first appearance is in the book of Acts: "The disciples were called Christians first at Antioch" (Acts 11:26).

epistles, salvation is a *gift* from God. Our good behavior is done out of *gratitude,* not just out of a sense of duty.

Paul's epistles run from Romans to the one-chapter book of Philemon. The long epistle of Hebrews (whose author is unknown) is addressed to "the new Hebrews"—that is, to all Christians, wherever they are. The final epistles, brief ones, are by James, Peter, John, and Jude. These books, and Hebrews, were written as *catholic* (meaning "universal") epistles addressed to Christians everywhere and circulated widely. Eventually all the epistles became catholic and are still read by Christians the world over.

Romans

Summary: Paul wrote this long letter to the Christians in Rome, a city he had not yet visited. The letter looks at how all people—Jews and non-Jews—have sinned and fall short of what God intended for us. All of us are dead in our sins but can be made spiritually alive through Jesus Christ, who sets us free from sin and enables us to fellowship with God. God gives us a new life by the Holy Spirit. This occurs not because of our own efforts but because of God's kindness. In his goodness he gives Christians different spiritual gifts, enabling us to work together for each other's good.

Challenges: None. Some readers may not like Paul's moral teaching (particularly on the sensitive topic of homosexuality), but Christians have considered this teaching to be authoritative for 2000 years.

Recommendations for reading: Don't miss a word. The 16 chapters here are some of the most important in the New Testament. Romans is the closest Paul came to writing a concise, organized "theology," a well-thought-out statement of basic Christian belief. And—hallelujah!—it is much briefer than most theology books.

1 Corinthians

Summary: Paul wrote this letter to the Christians in Corinth, a notoriously immoral city in what is now called Greece. Being a faithful believer in this decadent city wasn't easy. The church had signs of strain, with Christians arguing over beliefs and morals. Paul warns them against divisions and against allowing flagrant sinners to remain in the fellowship. Paul talks at length about Christian marriage and sexual morals. He explains the right way to worship together and about the various spiritual gifts Christians have. The glorious thirteenth chapter is the "love chapter," which describes love as the greatest gift. Chapter 15 gives a wonderful description of what Christians will be like in the afterlife.

Challenges: None. The modern world likes to argue with some of Paul's moral teaching (such as his words on homosexuality, 6:9). Paul's morality seems strict, but in our time, with so many people concerned about moral decay, this strictness should be a plus, not a minus.

Recommendations for reading: This letter is on a par with Romans. Read the entire letter, and make a point of rereading chapters 13 and 15 often.

2 Corinthians

Summary: Writing to the Corinthian Christians again, Paul discusses many issues, including the hardships he has experienced as an apostle. He assures his readers that these burdens are nothing compared to the glory awaiting all Christians. Paul defends his position as apostle, warning the readers against the many false apostles in the church.

Challenges: Some Bible scholars claim that 2 Corinthians is composed of more than one letter. But this is not a matter of concern to most Christian readers today.

Recommendations for reading: This epistle is not as "rich" as Romans and 1 Corinthians, but these passages warrant a rereading on occasion: our home in heaven (5:1-10), reconciling people to God (5:11-21), Paul's assurance that God's power is shown in human weakness (12:1-10).

Galatians

Summary: Paul wrote this letter to the Christians in Galatia, a province of the Roman Empire (in what is now Turkey). The Galatian Christians were being influenced by a group of people called Judaizers, who taught that Christians must obey all the Jewish religious regulations—circumcision, the kosher food laws, the observance of Jewish holidays, etc. Paul says loud and clear, "No! You're Christians. You're free from all those rules now. Don't let anyone impose these legalistic burdens on you." A key word in this letter is *freedom*. Christ sets us free from rules—not so we can run wild and be immoral, but so we can be kind, loving children of God. Instead of living by rules, we live by the Holy Spirit. We live a good life out of gratitude to God, not out of a feeling of duty and obligation and fear of punishment.

Challenges: None that are particularly notable, except for minor matters that scholars debate.

Recommendations for reading: Every word of this six-chapter letter should be read. It may seem to be focused on problems that are ancient history, but not so: Legalism has always been a problem among Christians, and the counsel in Galatians is a good antidote for it.

Ephesians

Summary: Paul wrote this letter to the Christians in Ephesus, a large coastal city in what is now Turkey. The letter deals with the church—not the building, but the community of Christians. They are one in Christ, all members of God's household. The Holy Spirit gives unity to all Christians. The Spirit enables Christians to live moral lives in an immoral world. Paul comments on how faith ought to affect relations between spouses, parents and children, masters and servants. He ends with a description of the "spiritual armor" that defends Christians against evil.

Challenges: Some Bible scholars doubt that Paul wrote Ephesians. They claim that the letter (in the original Greek text) is so different from Paul's other letters that it is probably by some other author. But many other scholars have no doubt that Paul is the real author. We know that Paul used secretaries who wrote down his words as he spoke, and it's possible that different secretaries might write Paul's words differently.

Recommendations for reading: Ephesians is only six chapters long, and it's all good reading. Its passages about Christian unity help break us out of the idea that you can be a solitary Christian.

Philippians

Summary: Paul wrote this warm, friendly letter to the Christians at Philippi, a city in Greece. It frequently uses the words "joy" and "rejoice," and Paul is joyful that the Philippians were so loving and kind. (Interestingly, this happy letter was written from prison. Perhaps Paul's spirits were lifted by remembering his dear old friends.) Paul claims that his persecutions are unimportant, since the new faith is growing rapidly in the world. The Philippians are encouraged to be humble, since Jesus himself was humble. The Christian goal is heaven, and everything earthly is worthless compared with that. Paul encourages the Philippians to hold to the faith, be joyful, and think on noble things.

Challenges: None.

Recommendations for reading: Philippians is short and easy to read. The chapter on humility (2) deserves rereading occasionally. This is a good letter to read when you're feeling down. It's a reminder to be content, even to rejoice, when things go wrong.

Colossians

Summary: Paul wrote this letter to the Christians at Colossae, a town in what is now Turkey. False teachers were leading the people away from Christianity, claiming they needed to add to the Christian faith by following special rules and diets and ceremonies and by worshipping angels. Paul encourages pure belief and warns against the immorality of the world. He also provides guidelines for moral living.

Challenges: Some scholars doubt that Paul wrote this letter (see the same note on Ephesians), but most agree that Paul did.

Recommendations for reading: Don't skip any part of this short letter. In our day of New Age teachings and various sects and cults, this letter (chapter 2 in particular) reminds us that Christ is enough, and we don't need to clutter the Christian life with useless, man-made rules.

1 Thessalonians

Summary: Paul praises the Christians in Thessalonica (a city in Greece) for being brave during persecution. Paul also gives counsel on a matter that had been causing them anxiety: When was Jesus returning, as he had promised?

Challenges: None, except that Paul seems to indicate that Jesus is returning to earth soon, which obviously (2000 years later) hasn't happened yet. Many parts of the New Testament predict that Jesus will return again to earth. That 2000 years have gone by doesn't mean the predictions were wrong (how would we know yet?), but that the authors clearly looked forward to this event. By the way, 1 Thessalonians was probably the first part of the New Testament to be written. Put another way, its words may be the oldest Christian writing in the world.

Recommendations for reading: At only five chapters, this book can be read quickly.

2 Thessalonians

Summary: Written shortly after 1 Thessalonians, this letter tells the Christians that, contrary to their expectations, Jesus may not come back for a while. He warns the people not to stop working while they await Jesus' return.

Challenges: None. This letter, like 1 Thessalonians, speaks about the return of Jesus to earth, and it sounds as if this will happen soon. It hasn't...yet.

Recommendations for reading: This book is a fast read with only three chapters. Second Thessalonians 3:16, almost at the end, is a beautiful blessing.

1 Timothy

Summary: This is a "pastoral letter," so called because it (as well as 2 Timothy and Titus) deals with how Christian pastors are to lead their churches. Paul warns the young pastor Timothy against false teachers. He instructs Timothy about worship, church officers, and lay members of the church. Paul warns against love of money and against rich Christians being cocky.

Challenges: Some scholars question whether Paul wrote this letter. In the original Greek text, the vocabulary is different from that which appears in Paul's other letters. This is natural, since Paul was addressing different issues. It is clear in the New Testament that Paul took a great interest in the works of his young colleagues, Timothy and Titus. Paul's words on women teaching in the church (2:9-15) have caused some minor controversy.

Recommendations for reading: This letter has some vital insights into how to conduct a church. The section on money (6:6-10,17-19) is a good summary of the Bible's teaching on that important subject.

2 Timothy

Summary: Again, Paul instructs the young pastor Timothy. He encourages him to stand fast in the faith. (In doing this, Paul gives a concise overview of some key points of the Christian faith.) Paul warns Timothy against people who claim to be Christians but aren't. He also reminds Timothy that all Scripture is "God-breathed" and is useful for training believers.

Challenges: None, except that, like 1 Timothy and Titus, some scholars doubt that Paul wrote this letter.

Recommendations for reading: This epistle, short as it is, should be read through. The encouragement in chapter 1 to be faithful is worth an occasional reread.

Titus

Summary: Paul wrote this letter to Titus, a pastor on the Greek island of Crete. He comments on the duties of pastors, elders, and deacons in the church.

Challenges: As with 1 and 2 Timothy, some scholars doubt Paul wrote this letter.

Recommendations for reading: Titus can be read quickly, and pastors and other church leaders ought to read it often.

Philemon

Summary: Paul wrote this letter to Philemon, a Christian friend whose slave, Onesimus, has stolen money from him and run away. Onesimus runs to Paul, then becomes a Christian. Paul sends Onesimus back to Philemon along with this letter. Paul begs Philemon to welcome Onesimus back as a Christian brother.

Challenges: None, except that some readers ask this obvious question: Why would Paul send the slave back to his master? Shouldn't a Christian oppose slavery? We can't go into more detail about this issue here, except to say that slavery was an accepted fact in the ancient world. Paul does emphasize that the Christian master and the Christian slave are brothers.

Recommendations for reading: Philemon is only one chapter long. It's a good read, and a touching letter. It shows a rather sweet side of Paul.

Hebrews

Summary: Jesus Christ, God's ultimate revelation to humanity, is superior to any past revelation, including Moses and the Old Testament law. Christ is the great High Priest, the one who mediates between God and man. Being both priest and sacrifice, he does away with the old Jewish system of animal sacrifices. The letter's final chapters discuss faith and some great role models of it, the way God disciplines his children, and the fact that the Christians' true home is in heaven.

Challenges: This is the "mystery letter"—we don't know the identity of the author, nor who exactly received the letter. Unlike the other epistles in the New Testament, this one names no author. Its style (in English or the original Greek) indicates that it is not by any of the other New Testament writers. (It is written in elegant Greek, which suggests the author was an intellectual type.) Besides this, we don't know exactly who "the Hebrews" were. By the time this letter was written, *Hebrews*, as a national or tribal term, was no longer used. Scholars like to argue about this. Did *Hebrews* means "Christians who had been reared as Jews," or could the term be symbolic—*Hebrews* meaning "God's chosen people"—that is, Christians? These questions haven't been answered, even after centuries of debate. But the early Christians saw fit to include this fascinating letter in its list of holy books, and readers throughout the centuries have found the letter inspiring.

Recommendations for reading: Don't skip anything. Hebrews, a long letter, deserves a good read-through. It is chock-full of quotations from the Old Testament, some of which may seem puzzling. But the book is full of beautiful passages about Jesus Christ and the role of faith in Christian life. Worth a reread is the famous "Faith Hall of Fame" in chapter 11. So is the passage on enduring hardship as a Christian (12:1-13).

James

Summary: Here is the first epistle named not for its recipients but for its author. James (who may have been the brother of Jesus) is more of a moral advisor than a theologian. He writes Christians everywhere about practical matters—enduring temptations, controlling anger, showing favoritism to the rich, controlling the tongue, praying for healing. Above all, this is the letter emphasizing that faith and good deeds go together—that is, a person with faith will do more than just talk about it.

Challenges: None. There are several men named James in the New Testament, but the scholars feel pretty certain that the author of this letter is James the brother of Jesus (who is mentioned in the book of Acts, chapters 15 and 21). Some people have claimed there is a conflict between James's teaching on faith ("faith by itself, if it is not accompanied by action, is dead"—2:17) and Paul's teaching that Christians are saved by faith alone and not by their good deeds. But there is no conflict. Both Paul and James agreed that both are essential in the Christian life.

Recommendations for reading: This is a short letter full of solid, practical advice—a basic how-to book for living the Christian life. The passage on taming the tongue (3:1-12) ought to be required reading—daily.

1 Peter

Summary: Peter, one of the more prominent of Jesus' 12 disciples, writes to Christians everywhere. He asks Christians to live holy lives, remembering that heaven is more enduring than this earthly life. He gives advice on living lives that will impress unbelievers. He especially looks at how Christians can endure suffering for their faith. And he gives advice on enjoying a loving Christian marriage.

Challenges: Some scholars have wondered how the apostle Peter, a simple fisherman, could have written a letter in such excellent Greek. Since authors often used secretaries in those days, we can assume Peter's aide might have been more skilled with words than Peter himself was. (Many a secretary today is more skilled with words than the boss giving the dictation.)

Recommendations for reading: First Peter is short and full of good advice. Particularly rewarding is the passage on suffering (4:12-19).

2 Peter

Summary: Peter wrote this epistle to Christians who were facing the challenge of false teachers. Peter predicts dire consequences for these people. He discusses the "day of the Lord," the time of Jesus' return to earth, and reminds Christians that they can look forward to a new heaven and new earth. This letter is the only place in the Bible that refers to another part of the Bible as being "hard to understand" (Paul's letters—3:16).

Challenges: None, although some scholars note that the styles of the Greek text in 1 Peter and 2 Peter are very different (which is easily explained—Peter could have used two different secretaries).

Recommendations for reading: These three chapters deserve reading.

1 John

Summary: John (the same one who wrote the Gospel of John) urges Christians to walk in the light of God's truth. He emphasizes love for God and fellow Christians rather than attachment to this world and our possessions. He gives advice on sorting out false teaching from true. Above all, he emphasizes love, the true test of whether we are a Christian.

Challenges: None.

Recommendations for reading: This short letter is a neglected treasure of the Bible. It is the "love letter" of the Bible, focusing especially on how believers ought to love each other. It ought to be read more often than it is.

2 John

Summary: John writes to "the chosen lady and her children" (verse 1) which may refer to a Christian community, and not an actual woman. As in 1 John, he emphasizes the importance of Christians loving each other and obeying God's commands.

Challenges: None.

Recommendations for reading: Though short, this letter with only 13 verses deserves a read-through.

3 John

Summary: John writes his "dear friend Gaius" (verse 1) about an arrogant Christian brother who is causing problems. He advises Gaius to imitate good instead of evil.

Challenges: None.

Recommendations for reading: This letter of 14 verses can be read through in one sitting.

Jude

Summary: Jude (who may have been a brother of Jesus) warns against false teachers, who have always been a problem for people of faith. Jude urges Christians to flee these teachers and to be kind to people wavering in their faith.

Challenges: None, except we aren't completely sure just who this Jude was. The name (it was actually Judas) is fairly common in the New Testament. The letter is *not,* of course, by the Judas Iscariot who betrayed Jesus. The letter was written by one of the *good* men named Judas.

Recommendations for reading: This is a short letter, and it does cover much the same ground as 2 Peter.

Revelation

Summary: Revelation is partly epistle (chapters 1–3), partly a vision of the end of time (the rest of the book). John, a Christian leader, writes to seven Christian communities in Asia (a Roman province, the area that is now called Turkey). Speaking on behalf of Jesus, he praises their good deeds and warns them against laziness and false teaching. Then, beginning in chapter 4, John describes visions of strange events taking place on earth and heaven—persecution of Christians, plagues on the earth, evil rulers, corrupt empires, and finally a triumphant Jesus returning to earth, the judgment of all the dead, and a happy ending complete with a new heaven and earth for God's people. The vision chapters are full of symbolic animals, people, and heavenly messengers. The book ends with the triumph of God and his people and the downfall of evil.

PEARLY GATES IN HEAVEN?

How many cartoons have you seen of St. Peter standing at the gate of heaven? Is that in the Bible? No. But according to the New Testament, heaven does have gates. And yes, they are *pearly* gates:

"The twelve gates were twelve pearls, each gate made of a single pearl" (Revelation 21:21).

And in case you were wondering, the same verse says that "the great street of the city was of pure gold, like transparent glass."

Challenges: What in the world does this mean? is the question readers ask again and again. John's letters to the churches (chapters 2–3) are clear enough, but the visions have puzzled readers for centuries. Did the visions forecast events in the lives of John's original readers in the Roman Empire? Events at the end of time, whenever that may be? Or do they report things that happen repeatedly—the persecution of God's people, with heaven as the destiny of every believer who dies? Ask ten Bible scholars or ten people off the street, and you'll get vastly different responses. But one thing is clear: The book predicts the final triumph of Christ and Christians over Satan and the powers of evil. The Christian's final destination is a heavenly reward free of pain or sorrow.

Recommendations for reading: Chapters 1–3 are pretty straightforward. The symbolism in the rest of the book may leave you feeling bewildered. But do read the final chapters (21–22), since they are an appropriate ending to the Bible.

9

Help at Your Elbow:

BASIC TOOLS FOR THE BIBLE READER

Y ou could benefit from reading the Bible without the help of any study aids. The Bible is accessible to everybody, and not just scholars and experts.

But 2000 years is a long time, and some parts of the Old Testament are much, much older than that. No matter how good and readable some of the modern translations are, there is much to gain from various books designed to help you understand the Bible. You could spend a fortune on these, but that isn't necessary. A few basic ones (many of them in paperback) will do the job quite well.

A Bible

First, let's consider the Bible itself. On pages 63-64 you'll find a discussion of various translations and their merits. If you have access to David Dewey's *User's Guide to Bible Translations* (InterVarsity Press, 2005), it provides useful information about the many translations available. Picking a translation is only one factor when choosing a Bible. Some other factors are...

Readability. Larger type is better than small type for most people. The tiny pocket testaments and pocket Bibles used to be popular, but unless you have the eyesight of a rabbit, these won't be very useful. (If your eyes are up to it, though, they do serve a nice purpose if you like to snatch a few minutes of reading when you're on the bus, waiting in the doctor's office, etc.) The large, heavy family Bibles that are still sold in stores and door-to-door usually have large and readable type (and pictures to boot). Unfortunately, most of them use the King James Version of the text—not the best translation for contemporary readers. And family Bibles aren't very portable, so you aren't likely to carry one with you when you travel. I have a suspicion that most family Bibles go unread. They are more often coffee-table decorations than anything else. (The next time you're in someone's home, check and see if there's dust on the family Bible's cover. Better yet, check the one in your own home.)

Durability. A good, solid binding makes for a longer-lasting Bible. Deluxe and gift Bibles often have elegant leather bindings and use very thin Bible paper. These are attractive, and people like to give them as gifts, but they can be expensive (though there are worse things you can spend money on than the Word of God). The thin pages in such Bibles are actually very durable. But if you think you'll be marking the pages with a pen or colored highlighter, you need to know that the ink can bleed through such paper. You can buy paperback Bibles, but they don't hold up too well. The worst problem with a paperback Bible is that it won't lie flat if you're studying at a desk or table. A clothbound Bible (with the binding you find on most hardback books) is a good choice. It will be more durable than a paperback and less expensive than a leather volume.

Writability. If you figure you'll be writing in the margins, choose a Bible that will give you room to do that. Many people (myself included) do this. Some Bibles have extra-wide margins just for this purpose. But if you're going to do any serious study of the Bible, you will want to go the extra step of always keeping a notepad near the Bible.

Groupability. If you know you're going to be involved in a church or study group that uses a particular translation, it makes sense to buy the same one the other folks are using.

Study aids. Most Bibles have a few study aids, usually in the back. These include a few maps of Bible lands, a brief concordance (more on concordances below), and perhaps a brief Bible dictionary. Some Bibles also include brief introductions to each of the 66 books.

Bibles with more extensive study aids are sold as study Bibles. See below for more information on them.

Red letters. Bibles called "red-letter editions" have the words of Jesus Christ in red. Some recent editions opt for green instead of red. I call this a nonessential option. Some people like it, others don't.

Color coding. A recent variation on the red-letter-edition Bible is the color-coded Bible. These feature color highlighting on passages related to a certain topic—say, green highlighting for passages concerning salvation, orange highlighting for passages concerning heaven and hell, etc. Some readers like this, others find it gimmicky. If you're the type who likes to underline or highlight, you'll probably find that these color-coded Bibles are more a hindrance than a help.

Bible Dictionaries

If you purchase just one study aid to go along with your Bible, you'll want to get a good Bible dictionary. These provide lists of names, places, and topics in the Bible, explain their meanings and point out where you'll find them in the Bible. A good Bible dictionary will also tell you how to pronounce Bible words, which is particularly helpful with Old Testament names. There are dozens of Bible dictionaries on the market, some of them being multivolume sets. The larger ones are intended for scholars, and they tend to be expensive. One of my personal favorites is *Young's Compact Bible Dictionary* (Tyndale House, 1989). You won't find a better pocket-size Bible dictionary. It's available in paperback, it's inexpensive, it gives the information you need and leaves out all the scholarly gibberish you don't need. *The NIV Compact Dictionary of the Bible* (Zondervan, 1999) is also good. Another favorite is *A Theological Word Book of the Bible,* edited by Alan Richardson (Macmillan, 1950). Don't let the title scare you off. This book includes every word of importance, not just words we think of as theological. It includes (just to name a few) *marriage, death, Christian, love, share, war, boast,* and hundreds of others. Every word and topic of importance is found, along with what the Bible says about that topic. My only complaint is that to save space, the editors used a *lot* of abbreviations in the book.

If you want something more scholarly and in-depth, *The New International Bible Dictionary* (Zondervan, 1999) is a good choice. It's large and bulky, but very thorough.

Concordances

This is an alphabetical listing of all the words (or just the key words) in the Bible, listed in the order in which they occur. Besides listing each chapter and verse where a word is found, the concordance will also show a few additional words from that passage to give you an idea of the context in which the word appears. So what purpose does it serve? Well, if you're looking for Bible verses on the subject of love, you could look up *love* in the concordance and find a list of all the verses containing that word, from Genesis to Revelation. (It would also refer you to related words such as *loved, loving,* etc.) This is, obviously, much easier than scanning the whole Bible itself in an attempt to find the places where the word *love* appears.

Concordances serve another purpose: You may have a Bible verse in mind but you can remember only one or two key words in it. By looking up one of those key words in the concordance, you will probably be able to find the verse you're looking for.

To give you a better idea of how a concordance works, here is a sample of what a concordance page might look like:

OPPOSES

And if Satan **o** himself	Mk 3:26
He **o** payment of taxes to Caesar	Luke 23:2
claims to be a king **o** Caesar	Jn 19:12
He **o** and exalts himself	2Th 2:4
"God **o** the proud	Jas 4:6
because, "God **o** the proud	1Pe 5:5

This is a complete list of verses in the New International Version that contain the word *opposes.* The verses are listed in the order that they occur in the Bible. Note that the books of the Bible are abbreviated (to save space, because concordances contain so much information). Note that each listing shows the portion of the verse that contains the word *opposes*. Note also that instead of repeating *opposes* in each case, the list simply uses an *o* (again, to save space).

Some Bibles have a small concordance in the back. These cannot be very thorough, owing to space limitations. On the other hand, you may not want to buy an exhaustive concordance because these can be expensive (and bulky). Some concordances even include Greek and Hebrew words, which is more than the average reader needs. You also wouldn't need an exhaustive concordance that lists all the verses with the words *and* and *the,* would you?

Several good, handy-size concordances are available. *The NIV Handy Concordance* (Zondervan, 1988) is designed for use with the New International Version. *Nelson's Comfort Print Bible Concordance* (Nelson, 1995) is designed for use with the New King James Version. As its name implies, it is set in a readable type. As noted below, concordances are also available in CD format, with some improvements over printed concordances.

Bible Commentaries

Commentaries basically explain the Bible text. They provide background information on the books of the Bible (who wrote which book, when, why) and explain the meaning of the Bible text verse by verse. Since commentaries are usually written by Bible scholars, they usually include informative details about the original languages and archaeology, helping to explain passages that may otherwise puzzle you. A good commentary is worth its weight in gold. Some of them are *too* weighty, however, filled with more information than you (or even other scholars) would ever need. For example, scholar Markus Barth managed to write a two-volume commentary on the letter to the Ephesians—a letter that, in my Bible, takes up a mere five pages.

There are one-volume commentaries (covering the entire Bible) and multivolume commentaries (you may find that these give you more information than you'll ever need). There are also commentaries on individual books of the Bible. A favorite one-volume commentary is *The New International Bible Commentary,* edited by F.F. Bruce (Zondervan, 1999). Large, with a library binding, it is based on the popular New International Version. It is scholarly and thorough. The best way to use it is to look up particular Bible passages you need explained. The introductory sections are probably too technical for most readers, but you can skip those. *The New Bible Commentary* (InterVarsity Press, 1994) is also good. There are dozens of excellent commentaries on individual books of the Bible, too many to mention here.

Study Bibles

A study Bible is a sort of marriage of Bible and commentary. Study Bibles have extensive footnotes and other aids to help explain the text. Their titles generally contain the words *Study Bible* or *Annotated.* (*Annotated* means "with notes," by the way.)

There are many study Bibles today. Consider just a few presently available: *The Seniors' Devotional Bible, The Couple's Devotional Bible, The Men's Devotional Bible, The Women's Devotional Bible, YouthWalk Devotional Bible, The Parenting Bible, Spirit-filled Life Daily Devotional Bible, Word in Life Study Bible, Life Application Bible, NIV Study Bible, Teen's Study Bible...*well, you get the idea. (No one has yet published *The Left-handed Thirty-year-old Republican's Bible,* but it's a possibility.) The ones mentioned here are all fine. A word of warning: Don't let the notes in a study Bible (or commentary) become a crutch for you. Footnotes and study helps are valuable, but try to interact with the Bible itself. Make sure you let your mind interact with the Bible text itself (and the Holy Spirit, if you believe what the Bible says about the Spirit being active as we study the Bible). It is true of commentaries and study Bibles that many brilliant people offer us their wisdom and insights about the Bible. But it is also true that the experts can sometimes be wrong. Learn from the scholars, but don't treat them as gods. They aren't.

Topical Bibles

Think of a topical Bible as a mega-concordance. A topical Bible lists all relevant Bible passages on a particular topic—for example, money, children, failure, etc. Instead of just briefly listing where those topics are covered, it actually gives the whole passage. So if you looked up *money* in a topical Bible, you would find all the Bible passages on that subject. (Note that the topical Bible lists *topics,* not words. The section on *money* would have passages dealing with money, even if the actual word *money* did not appear in that passage.)

Topical Bibles are wonderful. You can find, at a glance, every significant passage on every major topic. Topical Bibles are as addictive as popcorn. You'll find yourself continually browsing, turning from one interesting topic to another. Topical Bibles are usually hefty volumes, but they are a good investment. Buy one on the basis of the translation it uses. You can buy topical Bibles that use the New International Version, the New King James Version, etc.

Similar to topical Bibles are Bible promise books. These are designed to give aid and comfort by presenting Bible passages on key problem areas in life—marriage, children, career, ambition, money, etc. *The Complete Book of Bible Promises* (Tyndale House, 1997) is the most thorough, and *Biblical Quotations for All Occasions* (Random House, 1999) is good also.

Bible Histories

If you are curious about how Bible translators do their work, you might enjoy the American Bible Society's booklet *A Concise History of the English Bible.* This booklet, updated from time to time, is just what it says: a brief history of English Bible versions. It makes some interesting comparisons of the various versions available. A more detailed survey can be found in the multivolume *Cambridge History of the Bible in English,* which is very interesting. Benson

Bobrick's *Wide As the Waters: The Story of the English Bible* (Simon and Schuster, 2001) is quite good.

Bible Atlases

Does an atlas sound boring? Why would you even need maps of an area of the world you don't expect to drive through? Ah, but a good Bible atlas is more than maps. It shows the flow of biblical history, gives information on the movements of key Bible characters, and gives you the feel of place and time (reminding you that the events described in the Bible were real, not just religious fiction). A Bible atlas is not a necessity, and some are inexpensive. A favorite is *The HarperCollins Concise Atlas of the Bible* (HarperSanFrancisco, 1997). If you'd like a good reference book *and* something that looks nice on a coffee table, the *Reader's Digest Bible Atlas* is worth looking for. *The NIV Atlas of the Bible* (Zondervan, 1999) and the *Oxford Bible Atlas* (Oxford, 1985) are also good, but may be too technical and scholarly for most readers.

Books on Bible Ethics, Morals, Values

You can't do any better than Robertson McQuilkin's *Introduction to Biblical Ethics* (Tyndale House, 1995). Though it is an introductory -level volume, it is large and covers every conceivable moral issue related to marriage and family, racism, abortion, euthanasia, war, government, the media, work and leisure, etc. The author is a college president who knows how to think and write clearly.

Lewis Smedes's *Mere Morality: What God Expects from Ordinary People* (Eerdmans, 1983) is also excellent. As its title suggests, it is for ordinary people, not theologians.

C.S. Lewis's *Mere Christianity* (Macmillan, 1952) is still readable. Chapter 3, titled "Christian Behavior," is an excellent introduction to the Bible's view of morality and values. This book is one of the best investments you could ever make.

A Word About Buying Reference Books

Good reference books can be expensive. Some of the books

recommended above fit that category. Others (such as the excellent *Young's Bible Dictionary*) are both useful and inexpensive. You shouldn't have to spend a fortune on Bible study tools. Two or three basic reference books should serve you quite well. But if you are thinking of purchasing some of the larger books, check them out—literally, through a local library. If you find that a particular book is helpful to you, then you might want to purchase one for yourself. But it's better to make that decision after using the book for a few days—not just after flipping through one in a bookstore. Amazon.com and other Web sites now allow you to see sample chapters of books over the Internet.

Most of the books mentioned in this chapter can be purchased in regular bookstores, Christian bookstores, or on the Internet. If a book isn't in stock, a store can usually order it for you. But don't order any expensive book without first finding a copy you can browse through.

Computer Software

Technology marches on, and most Bible versions and Bible reference works are available now in CD-ROM format. Parsons Technology produces QuickVerse, which is available in several translations. QuickVerse is one of several Bible software programs that enable you to do more than just read text. You can also search for key words and names in the same way as you do with a concordance, but much faster. You could have your computer search for, say, all the verses that contain the word *husband.* You can also search for more than one key word simultaneously, which you can't do with a concordance. Let's say you are thinking of the Bible verse, "Love your neighbor as yourself." Where is that? You could look for this by telling the computer to search for all verses with the word *love.* But you would end up having to read through a lot of verses with that word. With the computer software, you can look only for verses that contain both *love* and *neighbor.* This is something a printed concordance can't do.

Some of the Bible CD-ROMs are a regular Bible library. Some, like BibleSoft PC Study Bible, contain not only the Bible text (sometimes more than one translation), but also aids such as a topical Bible, a Bible dictionary, maps, a concordance, etc. If you're computer-oriented to the point that you'd prefer working the computer to leafing through books, you might enjoy a product like this.

Audio Bibles

The Bible has been available in audio for years—first on cassettes, then on CDs. True, audio has limitations. You can't underline a favorite passage or write notes in the margins. But there is some value in bringing our ears as well as our eyes into absorbing the Bible. Teachers know that the two can reinforce each other. We learn best when we bring both eyes and ears into play.

Most religious bookstores have several versions of the Bible available on audio.

Bible Games

If the Bible is meant to be taken seriously (and it is), can it become a source of amusement? I raised that question in 1988, the year my *Complete Book of Bible Trivia* was published. The book was on the religious best-seller list for almost a year, went into numerous printings, and has been translated into (so far) five languages. I've concluded that people do like to "play" with the Bible. The serious side of this is that the Bible is seen as something approachable, something we need not keep our distance from. It is still holy, of course, but through quiz books and games we can approach it as user-friendly.

Most religious bookstores, and some secular stores as well, stock Bible games. There are many board games as well as computer games.

None of these games will actually get you into the deeper truths of the Bible. What they will do, aside from helping you pass the time in good clean fun, is reinforce some of the material you are absorbing through your regular study of the Bible. And a wonderful way to make the Bible approachable to kids is through Bible video games.